T0328445

Cambridge Elements

Elements in Corporate Governance
edited by
Thomas Clarke
UTS Business School, University of Technology Sydney

BOARD DYNAMICS

Philip Stiles
Cambridge Judge Business School

CAMBRIDGE
UNIVERSITY PRESS

CAMBRIDGE
UNIVERSITY PRESS

University Printing House, Cambridge CB2 8BS, United Kingdom

One Liberty Plaza, 20th Floor, New York, NY 10006, USA

477 Williamstown Road, Port Melbourne, VIC 3207, Australia

314–321, 3rd Floor, Plot 3, Splendor Forum, Jasola District Centre,
New Delhi – 110025, India

103 Penang Road, #05–06/07, Visioncrest Commercial, Singapore 238467

Cambridge University Press is part of the University of Cambridge.

It furthers the University's mission by disseminating knowledge in the pursuit of
education, learning, and research at the highest international levels of excellence.

www.cambridge.org
Information on this title: www.cambridge.org/9781108971393
DOI: 10.1017/9781108974875

© Philip Stiles 2021

First published 2021

A catalogue record for this publication is available from the British Library.

ISBN 978-1-108-97139-3 Paperback
ISSN 2515-7175 (online)
ISSN 2515-7167 (print)

Board Dynamics

Elements in Corporate Governance

DOI: 10.1017/9781108974875
First published online: June 2021

Philip Stiles
Cambridge Judge Business School
Author for correspondence: Philip Stiles, p.stiles@jbs.cam.ac.uk

Abstract: Boards of directors are at the apex of organisational decision-making and so are central in ensuring effective corporate governance. But boards are under increasing scrutiny due to the continuing prevalence of scandals and failures. Boards have been viewed as set up to fail because the demands placed upon them cannot effectively be delivered. Critics of current board arrangements point to time constraints, lack of adequate knowledge on the part of non-executive directors, and norms of deference within the board that prevent the effective flow of information and discussion. Others however, claim that the majority of boards operate effectively, and opinion is swayed by high profile cases of failure which are exceptions to normal practice. In this Element, I examine this tension and look at the board as a working group, one which has inputs (the characteristics of the board members themselves), dynamics (the internal workings of the board) and outputs (the accountability of the board regarding performance of the organisation and cohesion of the board itself). Through looking at the board as a group, the dynamics of how boards, and the potential for effective and ineffective operation, are highlighted. I conclude with outlining how the future of board dynamics may evolve.

Keywords: board of directors, unitary board, board composition, board dynamics, board performance, accountability

ISBNs: 9781108971393 (PB), 9781108974875 (OC)
ISSNs: 2515-7175 (online), 2515-7167 (print)

Contents

1. Introduction   1

2. Board Composition: Setting the Conditions for Dynamics   7

3. Dynamics and Process   23

4. Board Accountability   31

5. Renewing Boards of Directors   44

   References   58

1 Introduction

The role of the board is changing. A movement is developing which urges the board to focus on corporate purpose, and its contribution to social purpose. A number of major recent initiatives, notably the British Academy's work on 'The Future of the Corporation' (Mayer, 2018), and the US Business Roundtable's 'Statement on the Purpose of a Corporation' (Business Roundtable, 2019), have identified serious shortcomings in the way firms are run and have identified the need to reject shareholder primacy – the view that the only purpose of a business is to maximise shareholder returns – to argue for the idea of stakeholder governance and the promotion of purpose and trust.

The dangers of a shareholder-centric view, and its attendant problems with short-termism, have been made clear by these and other important contributions (Kay, 2012; Lawrence, 2017; Lipton, 2019; Sikka et al., 2018; World Economic Forum, 2016): increasing macroeconomic and financial instability, reductions in long-term competitiveness, fewer investments in innovative capability and decreased worker productivity.

These reports are the latest manifestations of an enduring debate about how to make governance more effective, and the role of the board within this. Some commentators argue that we have been here before. Concerns about short-termism have been a feature of the corporate governance landscape for a long time (see, for example, Marsh, 1993). Economic failure is nothing new; crises and scandals emerge regularly, prompting periodic calls for action (Clarke, 2010). Committees are set up, codes and various reforms are written, exemplars are lauded, transgressive companies are vilified. The board of directors tends to be singled out and viewed as suboptimal and in need of serious attention.

But this time feels different. The calls to action that opened this section suggest a sense of urgency and a common cause centred on the need to redress the problems caused by a shareholder-centric perspective, and the dangers of short-termism. For example, investors held shares on average for six years in the UK in the 1950s. That figure is down to six months now (Lawrence, 2017). This short-termism is mirrored in the USA. An important precursor to the Business Roundtable Statement of Purpose – Vitol's Principles 2.0' – argued that one of the principal reasons for the decline in numbers of public companies was the short-term perspective taken by investors that discouraged firms with a longer-term view (Commonsense Principles 2.0: para. 2).

Though the new governance initiatives differ as to whether regulation should be used to enforce a greater long-term value perspective (the British Academy work favouring a change in corporate law to place purpose at the heart of the objectives of the corporation, while the Business Roundtable Statement for

Purpose advocates a voluntary adherence to its principles based on an enlightened shareholder view), they share a common theme about the board of directors needing to raise its game. Directors are urged to provide effective contributions to ensure that the organisation follows purposeful objectives that have a long-term perspective (Lipton, 2019). The board therefore has a key role in ensuring that corporate purpose is enshrined within the organisation and its operations.

To deliver a corporate purpose that benefits society is wider than purely having a focus on corporate social responsibility. Rather it concerns how a board and the organisation can make a positive impact on environmental and social concerns within wider communities (Silverstein, McCormack, and Lamm, 2018).

A number of proposals have been put forward to support this view. First, boards have been asked to create a corporate purpose statement which highlights what the organisation does and why it does it (The Purposeful Company, 2018). A major board role would be to align the organisation's strategy, values and culture behind this statement of purpose (Mayer, 2018). This would be demonstrated by the board regularly communicating to stakeholders how the organisation is progressing in this alignment (Lipton, 2018).

Traditionally, social purpose and impact have been seen in terms of corporate philanthropy (for example, sponsorships) or as a targeted set of initiatives on particular issues (such as sustainability or diversity themes). More recent approaches have seen organisations approaching social purpose as an enterprise-wide commitment (Silverstein et al., 2018).

Second, a large part of delivering a corporate purpose that benefits society will be ensuring that the board attends to environmental, social and governance (ESG) issues. ESG is wide-ranging, encompassing employee relations and workplace practices, consumer and product safety and data security, environmental liabilities, supply chain and energy alternatives, board diversity, executive pay and business ethics. The Institutional Shareholder Services (ISS) review on ESG highlighted issues such as climate change, responsible consumption, data use, and discrimination as major concerns for boards (ISS, 2019: para. 4).

Managing ESG risk is a major element in the board's risk oversight role (Lipton, 2015). A number of organisations have created a separate board subcommittee to focus on the developing set of issues involved (Lipton, Niles, and Miller, 2018).

The board's potential for delivering social purpose is considerable. A board of directors is generally considered to perform two major roles (Hillman and Dalziel, 2003). The first is to "monitor the performance and behaviours of the

management and to ensure accountability to the owners and stakeholders"
(Hambrick, Misangyi, and Park, 2015: 323), including the review and approval
of strategy and the evaluation of the internal controls and risk (Daily, Dalton,
and Cannella, 2003; Judge and Zeithaml, 1992). This role is strongly informed
by agency theory, which asserts that the board is the key mechanism for aligning
the interests of the agent (the management of the company) with the principal
(the owners and/or stakeholders) (Fama and Jensen, 1983; Hermalin and
Weisbach, 2003). The second is a resource and service role, in which directors
provide advice to executives, and in addition facilitate contacts, knowledge and
resources between the organisation and its stakeholders (Hillman and Dalziel,
2003). This role is informed by the resource-dependence perspective, which
highlights the important benefits directors bring to the organisation, chiefly, new
information given through sharing advice from external sources, preferential
access to resources and knowledge from outside the organisation, and legitimacy (Hillman, Withers, and Collins, 2009: Pfeffer and Salancik, 1978).

Both agency theory and resource dependence theory view the board as
providing a mechanism of oversight and service to management, and as
a result having a positive effect on the governance and performance of the
firm. Other theories of the board, such as stewardship theory (Donaldson, 1990;
Davis, Schoorman, and Donaldson, 1997) and team production theory (Blair,
1995; Blair and Stout, 1999, 2011) challenge agency theory assumptions about
directors seeking to maximise their own interests, but concur on the board's
significance as the focus of monitoring and advice-giving to enhance decision-
making and accountability for the organisation.

The enactment of these roles depends on the contribution of independent non-
executive directors, defined as those who are not current or former company
employees or otherwise linked to the company or its managers (FRC, 2018).
This independence from the organisation allows them to have an objective view
of the organisation's strategy and operations, thus strengthening the monitoring
capability, and also to be in a position to bring new information and resources
and contacts external to the organisation (Westphal and Bednar, 2005).

Regarding social purpose, in the monitoring role, boards can enquire of
management whether the decisions and investments needed to fulfil their social
purpose, and the risks associated with them, are being enacted. In the advice-
giving role, boards can contribute to the strategic debate on social purpose,
providing new information on social purpose activities and trends from outside
the organisation and ensuring a broad discussion on the organisation's long-
term social impact.

However, while all this in principle sounds workable, boards find it difficult
to fulfil their roles. A recent influential review argued that boards may be in

a real sense 'set up to fail' (Boivie, Bednar, Aguilera, and Andrus, 2016). Some question whether directors have the ability to fulfil their roles adequately (Hambrick et al., 2015). For example, the extent of directors' other commitments may be overwhelming. At the level of the board, a powerful CEO can inhibit directors from actively making useful contributions, and the presence of certain board norms, such as deference and reciprocity, may severely limit directors' impact and value on the board. At the organisation level, most firms are characterised by complexity which makes understanding of the business (and information processing) very difficult indeed (Boivie et al., 2016; Hoppman, Naegele, and Girod, 2019).

The continuing presence of scandals in the corporate landscape, such as Carillion, HSBC, London Capital and Finance, Theranos, among many recent others, seems to support the view that the board faces an impossible task. A major theme of this Element is therefore to examine whether the board can manage these tensions and contribute effectively to delivering on the organisation's social purpose. I will focus on two key strands of debate. The first concerns structure. Since the thesis of the separation of ownership and control put forward by Berle and Means (1932), investors, policy makers, regulators, and governance scholars have emphasised the structural dimensions of governance, notably splitting the chair and CEO roles, ensuring a critical mass of independent directors, and introducing a raft of board committees to increase the scrutiny on management. Given the increasing demands for social purpose, it may be that the current structures do not allow the board enough latitude to pursue a broader purpose. We shall look (section 5) at a number of proposed reforms to the board in particular that may address this situation, including changing directors' duties to explicitly treat stakeholders on the same footing as shareholders (Lawrence, 2017; Sikka et al., 2018) and widening democracy on the board, beginning with the inclusion of employee directors. Experience of employee directors in European countries suggests that they result in better industrial relations and they prioritise longer-term performance horizons (Vitols, 2010).

The second key strand for debate focuses on the relational aspects of boards. A major reason for boards not fulfilling their roles effectively concerns the nature of interactions within the board. Work on behavioural governance suggests that 'widespread social norms for directors' behaviour often prevent corporate boards from fully exercising their control function on behalf of stakeholders' interests' (Westphal and Stern, 2006: 189) and cause non-executives to defer to executives and particularly the CEO.

On this view, boards are formed of individuals of varying backgrounds, personalities, motivations and ambitions, and the degree to which they come together behind a common board and organisational purpose will depend on how the relationships between them are managed. The behavioural view highlights how boards are socially situated and constituted, in contrast to agency theory, which says little about the actual dynamics that occur within a board (Westphal and Zajac, 2013). This point is often downplayed in talk of board reform, possibly because it reflects an unease that relationships cannot really be legislated for, and so remains an area where there can only be bland prescription and entreaties to behave well. This can be seen when researchers seek to link board structural characteristics to hard outcome measure of the firm, such as financial performance, The results of such research have yielded little (c.f. Desender, Aguilera, Crespi, and Garcia-Cestona, 2013), suggesting that the dynamics of the board and the ways directors make decisions have to be taken into account when considering the overall effect of boards on their organisations.

For boards to be effective and to deliver the imperatives of purpose-driven organisations, there must be a context of trust and collaboration between directors in order for information to be shared and processed. Directors must engage in behaviours that build confidence in each other's firm-specific and general business expertise (Kor and Sundaramurthy, 2009). There must also be a board culture within which discussions take place that can be characterised as challenging but supportive, with directors able to express dissenting views without fearing a loss of status. Through such dynamics, accountability can be developed, with accountability conceived here as stemming from a board which "questions intelligently, debates constructively, challenges rigorously and decides dispassionately" (Higgs Review, 2002: Annex C, para. 7). The importance of collaboration within the board rests alongside the need for directors to ensure control (Sundaramurthy and Lewis, 2003). This tension, which reflects the two roles of the board as monitor and advice-giver, thus can be mutually reinforcing, with informed directors whose expertise and engagement engender trust within the board, able to contribute ideas freely into discussions on strategy and operations, and this same trust provides confidence and acceptance that monitoring is carried out in a supportive and collegial manner (Lipton, 2019; Sumdaramurthy and Lewis, 2003; Roberts et al., 2005)

There must also be trust between directors and stakeholders, particularly concerning the need to deliver on purpose (Mayer, 2018). The board's role in setting the appropriate culture or 'tone from the top' is important here. The board's role in organisational culture and in risk culture represents a major dimension of its work.

In this Element I will discuss ways in which the board can enhance the relational elements of its work and examine how boards set the 'tone from the top' to develop culture and ultimately deliver corporate purpose with social impact.

The structure of the Element will reflect the perspective of the board as a particular kind of workgroup. Workgroups can be defined as 'collectives who exist to perform organisationally relevant tasks, share one or more common goal, interact socially, exhibit task interdependencies, maintain and manage boundaries, and are embedded in an organisational context that sets boundaries, constrains the team, and influences exchanges with other units in the broader entity' (Kozlowski and Bell (2003: 334).

For our analysis I adopt the classic structure of workgroup research – input, process, and output (Hackman, 1987; Marks, Mathieu and Zaccaro, 2001). In short, the inputs are board composition and tasks (section 2); the process is the board dynamics (section 3); and the outputs are board performance and cohesion (section 4), and I shall finish with thoughts about boards and the future.

I shall take this model's updated version, which is the input – mediator – output (IMO) (Ilgen, Hollenbeck, Johnson, and Jundt, 2005). In the input – process – output model, the behavioural processes are seen as the mediator between the inputs and the outcomes. The processes act as mechanisms that convert inputs into outputs. In the IMO model, the dynamic nature of members' interactions is taken into account and this focuses both on processes and emergent states.

This Element will examine primarily the board of directors within a corporation. Corporations employ thousands of people and their shares are held by the pension funds of the vast majority of individuals within countries. They have huge influence and power in the marketplace and often in their relationships with governments. How these companies are run really matters. Of course, there are organisations which also employ many people and which hold huge sway in national economies, which are not corporations, such as the civil service, the health service, the armed forces and the police, to name just a few. And naturally there are family firms and start-ups, and professional service firms with different governance arrangements. It is highly important that these organisations are governed well too. But the corporate form tends to be the major area of focus for research and policy from where other forms primarily take their lead, and so in this Element, this will be where our attention is centred. Similarly, this is not an Element about *comparative* governance. I shall touch on the merits or otherwise of dual boards that are found in certain countries, and indeed I will advocate that the principle of employee representation, as found in a number of jurisdictions, should be instigated in the UK and the US. But the focus will be on the unitary board of directors. Lastly several areas which are important for board behaviour, such as the nature of financial markets, the role of regulators, the disciplinary power of analysts and the media, insolvency law and tax law, the market for corporate control, and executive pay, I can only touch on in the bounds of this Element. Each are deserving of an Element in their own right.

Our next section will focus on the inputs to the board, and examine board composition. This is important since the mix of directors regarding their knowledge, the time they can give to their duties, the weighting between executive and non-executive directors, and the diversity within the board, will all strongly influence the nature and dynamics between board members. For example, if the non-executive directors have very similar demographic attributes to the CEO, this may result in a set of dynamics which may be very different from a board where the demographics were more dissimilar. With board process, how the board conducts itself with regard to meetings, agendas and topics discussed, and how this process is led (primarily by the Chair) will also have significant influence on the dynamics of the board.

2 Board Composition: Setting the Conditions for Dynamics

The fundamental ingredient in board dynamics is the combination of skills, behaviour, knowledge and attitudes of the directors. Like all work groups, the selection of members and the composition of the group overall will have strong implications for the dynamics of the collective. With the movement toward corporate purpose and social impact, this theme has become more important than ever. For example, the 'New Paradigm' states that:

> *The composition of a board should reflect a complementary diversity of thought, background, skills, experiences and tenures. The board of directors should develop a system for identifying diverse candidates, including women and minority candidates, and for effectively integrating new members into the board dynamic'*. (Lipton, 2019: 43).

The call for greater diversity reflects the need to broaden the thinking within the board to include a longer-term perspective and stronger and more insightful relationships with stakeholders. Recent data suggest that there has been progress in this area.

In 2019 the major headhunting firm Spencer Stuart published their annual Board Index survey and announced that women, and men from minority backgrounds (defined as African-American/Black, Hispanic/Latino or Asian) constituted a majority of the cadre of new intake of directors (Spencer Stuart US, 2019). However, female representation in key roles overall remains poor. In the UK, just 3.3% of Chairs are women and 4% of CEOs (Spencer Stuart UK,

2019), while in the US, women currently have only 6% of CEO roles in S&P 500 companies (Catalyst, 2020). For ethnicity, the picture is no better; only 5% of CEOs of major firms in the UK and US are from an ethnic minority background and there are no women CEOs who are from an ethnic minority.

So only two cheers for greater diversity on boards. In addition, overall, high-quality board members seem to be scarce, due to a number of factors such as regulatory pressure, concerns about time commitment, and possible reputational risk (Risso-Gill, 2018).

These figures tell an interesting story. After decades of opaque processes of director selection resulting in remarkably similar profiles on boards of directors, things are beginning to improve. But the improvement is very slow and from a very low base. In addition, problems about finding the right talent, and having the right processes to acquire it, remain. This reflects the very thorny nature of board composition and selection.

This is the foundation of board dynamics and also one of the least well understood aspects in corporate governance research. In this section I shall look at these elements and examine what they mean and what the implications are for boards and governance. I organise the section as follows. First, I shall look at board structure, examining key elements such as the difference in governance approaches between countries, the composition of board committees, issues of board size and the requirement for independence. Then I shall discuss the human and social capital dimensions of boards, and introduce ideas on board selection, succession and diversity. Let us begin with the issue of board structure.

2.1 Board Structure

There are two broad versions of board structure: the unitary (or one-tier) board, primarily seen in the UK, USA, Australia and Canada; and the two-tier board, chiefly seen in Asia, mainland Europe and Latin America. The characteristic of the unitary structure is that executive and non-executive directors work together on one board. The unitary board thus would typically include (i) the CEO, who runs the organisation and leads the executive group; (ii) the executive directors; (iii) a Chair, normally a non-executive director, who runs the board of directors; (iv) the independent or non-executive directors; and (v) a senior independent director, (SID), a position introduced following the Higgs report (2002), who is a non-executive director providing a conduit between the board and stakeholders should normal routes of communication between investors and the Chair and/or CEO become problematic, or if a rift occurs between CEO and Chair (Block and Gerstner, 2016; FRC, 2018, IOD, 2018). There is also usually a company secretary, who ensures that the process of the board – the provision of the agenda and the board papers, the taking of minutes and giving advice on procedural issues – are carried out effectively.

Under the UK Corporate Governance Code, at least half of the board (excluding the Chair) should be independent directors, ideally with a diversity of backgrounds (FRC, 2018). The Code also states that the Chair and CEO roles should not be held by the same person, and the Chair should not be a former CEO of the firm. In the USA, which also has a unitary board structure, the CEO tends to be sole executive on the board, with the rest of the board comprising independent directors. Approximately half of boards in the USA have separated the roles of CEO and Chair, with the other 50% having a combined CEO and Chair role (Spencer Stuart US, 2019).

The debate about the merits of splitting the CEO and Chair has a long lineage (Dalton and Dalton, 2011). The arguments for the CEO and Chair positions being held simultaneously by one individual (the CEO duality perspective) is that it provides a unified focus of leadership and this can be reassuring both for managers within the organisation also for external stakeholders. This perspective derives support from work in organisation theory on leadership and legitimacy (Finkelstein and D'Aveni, 1994). Proponents of splitting the roles draw on agency theory to argue that CEO duality may encourage the entrenchment of the CEO, which would dramatically reduce the ability of the board to monitor and discipline effectively (Fama and Jensen, 1983). A further argument against combining the two roles is that they are fundamentally different positions, and joining them in one person risks either task overload or a gap in capabilities, resulting in an ineffective board (Demb and Neubauer, 1992). Numerous studies have sought to determine which structure has the most positive outcomes for corporate performance, but no substantive relationship has been demonstrated (Dalton and Dalton, 2011). Nevertheless, the arguments against CEO duality have generally prevailed and it is only really the USA where a significant proportion of listed companies have the roles combined.

In a two-tier board structure, a management board of executive directors, responsible for the company's strategy and its implementation, is monitored by a distinct supervisory board, comprising non-executive directors, who review the strategy and the overall health of the organisation for shareholders. The supervisory board is responsible for the appointment (and the remuneration level) of the management board members. The supervisory board itself is appointed by the shareholders of the organisation. There is a prohibition against an individual having a seat on both boards (Block and Gerstner, 2016).

The two approaches to board structure largely reflect the pattens of economic and political differences that occur between nations. Research in this area has been largely informed by the Varieties of Capitalism tradition (Hall and Soskice, 2001), which makes the distinction between Liberal Market Economies (LMEs) and Coordinated Market Economies (CMEs). In LMEs, firms coordinate their activities primarily through "competitive market arrangements" which are "characterised by the arm's-length exchange of goods or services in a context of competition and formal contracting.' (Hall and Soskice, 2001: 8). In CMEs, "firms depend more heavily on non-market relationships to coordinate their endeavours with other actors and to construct their core competencies." (Hall and Soskice, 2001: 8)

In LMEs, reliance on market-based mechanisms produces a premium on transparency for information, high disclosure, an active takeover market, an active private equity market, and equality of treatment to shareholders. It also emphasises a market relationship between the individual employee and the firm, giving management a high degree of freedom to hire and fire in order to allow the firm to be adaptable.

Share ownership is dispersed in LMEs, and this entails a large degree of shareholder passivity, since each shareholder only has a relatively small stake, which is usually part of a portfolio of other investments, and so the incentive to monitor or be generally involved with an individual company is low. This separation of ownership and control has historically been addressed by an "arms-length" mode of governance which does not rely on direct intervention by shareholders but instead looks to mechanisms such as independent oversight by the board to ensure the interests are alignment between owners and management.

CMEs, by contrast, have a less-dispersed shareholding and are characterised by organisations operating in collaborative complex networks. Ownership is more concentrated, with banks, families and state finance being dominant, and as a result, there is a limited market for takeovers or private equity, and limited disclosure, with the majority shareholders having far better information and benefits relative to minority shareholders. For CMEs, organisations rely much less on finance sourced through equity markets or other publicly available and transparent financial data, and more on credit-financing, sourced through "dense professional and business networks with strong trust levels that have a more long-term focus" (Hall and Soskice, 2001: 9).

The implications for board structure are clear. For CMEs, the presence of large block holders in capital markets brings less liquidity in these markets and increases the incentive for these investors to have direct control, since they cannot disburse their stakes in firms quickly. CMEs tend to have two-tier boards, with the supervisory board including representatives of relationship partners such as banks, suppliers and firms who are working in collaboration.

Importantly, workers will be represented on the board too. Though the way representation is achieved varies between countries, the usual way is for employees to directly elect representatives to the board. For example, in Germany, the supervisory board, due to co-determination rules, has either one-third, or one half of the board made up of employee representatives, depending on the size of the organisation, all employee-elected. (Block and Gerstner, 2016).

The LMEs tend to have unitary boards, reflecting the market driven, arm's length approach, with independence being the chief characteristic of the board rather than representation. The LME has its roots in the idea of shareholder primacy. In contrast, within CMEs, stakeholder primacy is enshrined.

The single-tier board and the two-tiered board both have strengths and weaknesses. The single-tier board usually has better information flow and has faster decision-making potential. Also, it is more likely that non-executives will have greater knowledge and engagement with the organisation. The two-tier board, however, is not conflicted in being involved in the decision-making process while also having to oversee that process (Block and Gerstner, 2016).

There is no definitive research to support the superiority of either system in terms of organisational performance. A criticism of the varieties of capitalism literature, along with other broadly similar approaches such as the National Business Systems perspective (Whitley, 2007), is that "they are often not well-suited for characterizing the increasingly significant group of newly-developed, emerging, and developing economies" (Fainsshmidt, Judge, Aguilera, and Smith, 2018: 307). But the rationale for the differences between the two systems remains unaffected. In this Element I will focus on the one-tier (unitary) board.

2.1.1 Board Committees

In addition to the main board, there is also the board committee structure to consider. There are three statutory committees for listed companies; the audit, remuneration and nomination committees.

The audit committee is responsible for ensuring the integrity of financial reporting and the audit process, and the company has sound internal financial control systems and systems for the control of non-financial risks (FRC, 2018). This includes ensuring the external auditor is independent and objective. The audit committee should comprise solely independent non-executive directors, which should not include the Chair of the board, and these members should be knowledgeable about the business environment, and of whom one has accounting or financial management expertise (FRC 2018). Without such knowledge, the oversight role of the committee will be reduced in credibility. The audit committee in large companies should meet no fewer than three times a year, with some meeting considerably more often, between six and ten times per year (FRC, 2018).

The role of the remuneration committee is to set and agree with the board the terms and process for the remuneration of the CEO, the Chair and the executive directors (FRC, 2018). The recommendation of the UK Corporate Governance Code is for the remuneration committee to comprise at least three independent non-executives (or in the case of smaller companies, two). The Chair of the board can be a member, but only if they were independent on appointment, and they cannot chair the committee (FRC, 2018). Remuneration committees should meet at least twice per year, once close to the year end to review the directors' remuneration report, which, for quoted companies is submitted to shareholders for approval at the AGM (FRC, 2018a).

The nomination committee leads the board appointments process (FRC, 2018). In particular the committee identifies and recommends candidates to the board (Kaczmarek, Kimino, and Pye, 2012). The nominations committee also makes judgements on the re-nomination of current directors who may be retiring by rotation. Best practice guidelines suggest nominations committees should meet at least twice a year (FRC, 2018). The nominations committee will also have responsibility for ensuring the drawing up and maintenance of succession plans for the board and the executive directors. The nominations committee would comprise a majority of non-executive directors.

The committee structure is present in most major jurisdictions, including those with two-tier structures. Many organisations have other committees set up in addition to the mandatory three. In the UK, the proportion of listed companies with more than three committees is at 56.7% (Spencer Stuart UK 2019). The most common of these additional committees are the Corporate Social Responsibility committee, which is present in just over a fifth of companies, and the risk committee, seen in 17% of companies, the vast majority in banks and other financial services organisations (Spencer Stuart UK 2019).

2.1.2 Board Size

In the UK the average size of the board for FTSE 150 companies is 10.3 (Spencer Stuart, UK, 2019). In the US the average for S&P 500 is 10.8 board members (Spencer Stuart, US, 2019). For German boards of major organisations, the average is 23, though this number is for the supervisory board where there is a large number of stakeholder representative directors; the management board has an average of 10 (Spencer Stuart US, 2019). Smaller boards are able to communicate more easily, have greater flexibility in anticipating or responding to change, experience less 'free riding' and be at less risk of developing factions or faultlines which could hamper the monitoring role of the board (Hackman, 1987; Katzenbach and Smith, 1993).

2.2 Director Independence

In the unitary board structure, the non-executive directors are largely independent directors. In the UK, the Combined Code (FRC, 2018: provision 10) states that a non-executive director is independent if the following conditions are not met: namely, if a director:

- is or has been an employee of the company or group within the last five years;
- has, or has had within the last three years, a material business relationship with the company, either directly or as a partner, shareholder, director or senior employee of a body that has such a relationship with the company;
- has received or receives additional remuneration from the company apart from a director's fee, participates in the company's share option or a performance-related pay scheme, or is a member of the company's pension scheme;
- has close family ties with any of the company's advisers, directors or senior employees;
- holds cross-directorships or has significant links with other directors through involvement in other companies or bodies;
- represents a significant shareholder; or
- has served on the board for more than nine years from the date of their first appointment.

In the UK, 96% of non-executives at British-based FTSE150 firms qualify as independent (Spencer Stuart UK, 2019). Under the New York Stock Exchange rules, independent directors are deemed to be those who have 'no material relationship with the listed company.' In the US, 84% of S&P 500 company boards have independent directors (Spencer Stuart US, 2019).

In two tier jurisdictions, particularly those with employee co-determination, the requirement for independence is less, due to the presence of employee representatives and stakeholder representatives on the supervisory board. This reflects the role of directors in these jurisdictions as representative of stakeholders, rather than as providing independent oversight (Block and Gerstner, 2016).

2.3 Board Human and Social Capital

I mentioned earlier that boards are supposed to have a combination of the right skills, behaviour, knowledge and attitudes to ensure the board can perform effectively. To put this slightly more formally, boards need to have positive human and social capital. Human capital refers to the skills, behaviour, knowledge and attitudes themselves (Becker, 1975; Westphal and Fredrickson, 2001). Social capital refers to 'the sum of the actual and potential resources embedded within, available through, and derived from the network of relationships possessed by an individual or social unit. Social capital thus comprises both the network and the assets that may be mobilised through that network' (Nahapiet and Ghoshal, 1998: 243). Through these resources from director networks, knowledge and information can be developed and transferred and integrated into the organisation, making for greater decision-making effectiveness (Burt, 1992). Empirical evidence shows that the human and social capital of directors are linked to the effectiveness of the board (e.g., Carpenter and Westphal, 2001; Hillman and Dalziel, 2003; McDonald, Westphal, and Graebner, 2008). I shall look at human capital and social capital in turn.

2.3.1 Human Capital

The lists of capabilities required by directors are numerous and subject to variability but at their core, they have a high number of common aspects. Recently this has been summarised in terms of directors needing five 'intelligences' (Hesketh, Selwood-Taylor, and Mullen, 2020), which are: financial, strategic, relational, role, and cultural.

The leading aspect is financial expertise. Research on board performance has consistently highlighted this feature as important for boards. Financial expertise has been positively linked to board and organisational performance. For example, investors react positively to financial experts being appointed to a firm's audit committee (Davidson, Goodwin-Stewart, and Kent, 2005). Strategic thinking requires being able to see the bigger and longer-term picture from an organisation-wide perspective. Relational intelligence indicates an ability to build effective working relationships with peers. Role intelligence refers to the understanding of one's place on the board and not to overstep this (e.g. a non-executive encroaching on executives' decision-making domain). Cultural intelligence is to be a part of developing a favourable board environment that encourages debate and performance.

Regarding the types of people who are most valued as non-executive directors, the most highly sought after is a CEO. According to Spencer Stuart (2019) 38% of directors are either current of former CEOs, chairmen, presidents or

COOs. Not surprisingly, CEOs running successful organisations will be invited to more board appointments than CEOs of under-performing firms. (Fich, 2005). Industry experience for a non-executive director is also highly valued, with studies showing that directors complement and supplement the experience of the executive cadre (Kor and Misangyi, 2008; Kor and Sundaramurthy, 2009).

Political experience can also be important, with several studies showing that the political experience of a director to be valuable to the board (e.g. Hillman, 2005). General business expertise is also a sought-after characteristic (Kroll, Walters, and Le, 2007). However, research by Almandoz and Tilcsik (2016) showed that in contexts where decision-making is significantly uncertain, having more domain experts on the board can reduce the quality of its decision-making process.

2.3.2 Social Capital

A director's social capital is an important resource for the board and the firm as a whole (Hillman and Dalziel, 2003). The resource dependence perspective asserts that directors can connect the firm to its environment through their networks (Hillman, Cannella and Paetzold, 2000). This external perspective on social capital is crucial in a board's relationship with stakeholders outside the host organisation. It is augmented by directors' internal social capital, which are the links and networks within the host organisation that allow the board to work together effectively. Both categories of social capital influences director selection.

Significant empirical research supports the benefits of both forms of social capital to the effectiveness of the board (Kim and Cannella, 2008). Kor and Sundaramurthy (2008) showed external social capital in the form of multiple directorships increased growth in high-tech firms through providing resources to the host firm. External social capital also has been shown to increase trust and engagement between the organisation and its stakeholder groups (Maak, 2007). The internal social capital of directors similarly is beneficial to the organisation, particularly regarding trust (Kim and Cannella, 2008). Social capital is also significant for influence within the board. Directors who have strong relationships among board members and who in addition meet outside the board have increased influence in how decisions are made within the board. (Stevenson and Radin, 2009).

Despite the benefits of social capital, there are drawbacks. These would include the possibility that drawing on social networks for knowledge acquisition or for selection of directors may risk developing a homogeneity of belief and value systems which can constrain the effectiveness of the board. We see the double-edged nature of social capital most clearly when looking at the issue of board selection, to which we now turn.

2.4 Board Selection

A traditional approach to selecting board members revolves around utilising board social capital or networks. A strength of this approach is that it can be efficient, since boards operate largely on consensus (we will explore this issue in section 3) and appointing individuals with whom there is already a connection can reduce the costs of coordination and lower the learning curve for the new individuals joining the board (Cai, Nyugen and Walkley, 2020). This argument, called the 'coordination hypothesis', suggests that appointing a director within the network of other board directors enhances the effectiveness of the organisation, and considerably so in the context of complex uncertain conditions. This argument would support a greater stewardship approach to the board and downplay the importance of independence in a director in favour of better coordination and collaboration. Stewardship theory questions agency theory assumptions that agency costs will accrue if appropriate control mechanisms (such as a cadre of independent non-executives) are not in place to prevent self-serving and opportunistic behaviour on the part of agents. Stewardship theory suggests that in a number of contexts, managers and executives are best characterised as motivated by pro-organisational goals and acting as good stewards of the firm (Davis, Schoorman, and Donaldson, 1997).

Research on the coordination hypothesis (Cai et al., 2020) examined the prevalence and consequences of director recruitments from the networks of their board members, and found that 94% of the director nominees at S&P 500 firms are selected from a panel of individuals with first-degree connection (people with whom the incumbent board or CEO has worked with in director and/or executive capacity) or second-degree connections (who have worked with or been on the same board with one of the direct connections) to the incumbent board.

A second reason why boards tend to select in their own image comes from research on the attraction-similarity hypothesis. On this view, demographic similarity is seen to influence selection decisions, in particular applicants with demographic similarity to the selector are perceived to be of higher quality than those with less similarity (Westphal and Zajac, 1995).

However, it is clear that through such processes a possible consequence is that the board can develop a similarity of perspective that may be damaging, in light of changing environmental contexts, when different views and challenges could be extremely valuable. This 'homophily hypothesis' (Cai et al., 2020) suggests that boards can be blindsided by a homogeneous set of directors and would benefit from widening the number of perspectives and increasing diversity within the board overall.

Governance regulators and reformers have emphasised the role of the nominations committee in ensuring good selection and succession practice, and it is to this we attend to next.

2.4.1 The Nominations Committee

In the UK and the US, in theory, shareholders elect directors. Typically, however, shareholders find it difficult to perform this responsibility, due to time or knowledge constraints and to the spread of their shareholdings in other organisations. In reality therefore, it is the board, acting as the shareholders' representative, that selects directors. In most cases the process of selection will be through candidates being identified and screened by a nomination committee composed almost entirely of independent non-executive directors (Eminet and Guedri, 2010; Hoskisson, Castleton, and Withers, 2009; Monks and Minow, 2011).

Under the UK Corporate Governance Code, (principle B.2) there should be 'a formal, rigorous and transparent procedure' for the appointment of new directors. The composition of the nomination committee should be 'predominantly non-executives' and should be chaired by one of the independent non-executives or by the company Chair. The CEO can be a member, given that the nominations committee is also responsible for making appointments for executive directors, in addition to non-executive appointments.

Boards have to assess the balance of skills, knowledge and experience within the membership and ensure that there is a succession plan in place and the continual revitalisation of the board is carried out.

The nomination committee's role also includes the committee's evaluation of the board's own performance. Board are required to conduct a board performance self-evaluation at least annually, both under NYSE rules, and also for Combined Code rules (FRC, 2018). While there has been a good deal of prescriptive advice about how such reviews should take place, the role of the nomination/governance committee in this process has yet to be explored fully. I will look at board evaluation in section 4, when I look at issues of performance.

2.4.2 CEO Succession

One major aspect of the selection process concerns CEO succession. There are three main elements underpinning this process. First, boards identify the roles and responsibilities for the position. Second, boards determine what are the key skills needed to take the organisation forward. Third, the board can set developmental opportunities for the prospective candidates that will support an effective transition (Schepker, Nyberg, Ulrich and Wright, 2018).

This process looks straightforward yet succession in general remains high on the list of board roles that are typically ineffective (ICGN, 2018)

The major problem with CEO succession is the uncertainty around the process and the potential of adverse selection. Boards usually do not know enough about the skills and capabilities of possible candidates within the firm or outside the firm. Further, there may be uncertainty about the strategic needs and direction of the organisation which the new candidate will have to address (Zajac and Westphal, 1996; Zhang and Rajagopalan, 2004).

In many cases, boards rely on the CEO to highlight appropriate candidates. But this task may be difficult even for them since many capabilities are difficult to codify (Wiersema, Nishimura, and Suzuki, 2018). Also, the process may be compromised by political and personal emotions of incumbent CEOs, who may seek to appoint an heir apparent who will continue their strategic direction rather than open the choice to a range of other candidates. The uncertainty around CEO succession is typically reflected in the reaction of investors to the announcement. Increased share price volatility continues for around two years as firms undergo a succession process (Wiersema et al., 2018).

Some succession of course is not a 'handing over' or 'baton-passing' process but an abrupt departure due mostly to the dismissal of the CEO because of underperformance of the CEO and /or the firm or concerns about their leadership style or ethical behaviour. This puts additional uncertainty on the board as now it is working in crisis mode to establish the reasons behind the departure as well as to ramp up the recruitment process when the firm is under intense scrutiny. This scenario underlines the importance of succession being a proactive multiyear process connected strongly to a coherent system of leadership development through the organisation (Bjornberg and Feser, 2015).

In addition to looking at internal candidates, boards will want to ensure a rigorous succession process by looking at external candidates also (Conference Board, 2019). This comparison process reduces the risk of bias and also opens up new possibilities for candidate selection (Schepker, Nyberg, Ulrich, and Wright, 2018). This will naturally be the case if the board is leaning towards an outsider. Research on the insider and outsider issue is mixed regarding the impact on performance. Generally, it seems that the appointment of an insider is most common, since they offer continuity, have deep knowledge of the organisation, and are reasonably well known by the board, so decreasing the possibility of adverse selection (Conference Board, 2019). However, organisations tend to hire external CEOS when they are facing a difficult operating environment and there is a clear need for change (Parrino, 1997). Stock market reaction to an external appointee is positive in such contexts in the hope that the new CEO will effect change (Hayes and Schaefer, 1999).

To examine possible candidates from the external labour market, usually the board will work with an independent search firm to develop a list of nominees. They would provide an initial selection of candidates after which the board develops a shortlist and undertakes interviews and other means to ascertain the right person.

Through all this the board takes control. Given the complexity of this event, and the potential for conflicts of interest with management and potentially shareholders, the major part of the work in finding a CEO successor would be undertaken by the nomination committee. The committee would usually have responsibility for the whole process and at the end of their deliberations, would present their assessment to the main board.

2.4.3 Board Diversity

A major element for consideration within nomination committees is the selection of directors under the criterion of diversity. Diversity has strong benefits through a broadened range of board resources (such as knowledge, skills, and perspectives) (Williams and O'Reilly, 1998). Nomination committees try to ensure that the make-up of the board is optimal regarding functional and professional capability. Diversity is a highly important element in this process. Research suggests that greater cognitive variety within the board will increase the number of options considered and make it more likely that those options will be discussed in depth, thereby making the decision-making process more effective (Rindova, 1999). But research on demographic diversity has shown equivocal results regarding diversity and performance (Klein, 2017). Some scholars have highlighted that boards which reflect their company's employee and customer demographics can be much more responsive to the needs of these key stakeholders (Hillman, 2005).

However, two meta-analyses on the relationship between female board representation and performance found either no relationship or a very weak positive relationship. Post and Byron (2014) examined 140 studies of board gender diversity ranging across 90,000 firms from upwards of 30 countries, and found a tiny positive effect (almost close to zero), while Pletzer and colleagues (Pletzer, Nikolova, Kedzior, and Voelpel, 2015) looked at 20 studies that focused on board gender diversity and firm financial performance, and found no effect. A meta-analysis involving 146 studies examining the relationship between CEO gender and long-term company performance also found a very small positive effect (.007) (Jeong and Harrison, 2016).

With ethnic diversity, there are far fewer studies to examine, and the picture is again mixed (Larcker and Tayan, 2016). A number of studies find the relationship between minority directors and firm performance is positive (Carter, Simkins and Simpson, 2003; Miller and Triana, 2009) whereas others show no association (Carter et al., 2010; Guest, 2019)

Of course, the lack of a clear association with both gender and ethnic minority directors may rest with the general problem in identifying direct effects to firm performance from structural characteristics. Or it may signify that women or ethnic minority directors may differ in demographic characteristics but may not differ significantly in their cognitive diversity, given they will have been chosen on the basis of professional managerial and executive capabilities which may produce similarity of cognitive framing.

2.4.4 Quotas

A benefit of introducing quotas is that they focus board attention on ways to increase the search for the required candidates. A number of countries – Belgium, France, Germany, Iceland, India, Israel, Italy, Norway, Pakistan and Spain – have introduced, for publicly-listed firms, target quotas for women between 30% to 40% on the board. For Belgium, France, Italy and Norway there are sanctions for non-compliance, including dissolving the company. In other countries, there are soft law provisions, with no sanctions. In the UK, there are guidelines only (Economist, 2018). In the US, California introduced quotas in September 2018. These stipulated that, for publicly-listed firms, at least one woman should be on the board. They were the first state to do so, and are due to be followed by Illinois, Massachusetts, New Jersey, and New York.

The evidence for the effect of quotas on performance is mixed (Ferrari et al., 2018); nevertheless, this does not impugn the moral case for reducing inequality in the distribution of board positions. However, opponents of quotas argue on the grounds that there is a risk of appointing people who may be unable to perform the role to an appropriate level. Studies following Norway's pioneering decision to introduce 40% quotas found that while the gender quota was beneficial for the presence of women at the very top, there was little or no effect of this helping women lower down within organisations (Bertrand et al., 2019). Also, in Norway there was evidence of companies delisting following the introduction of the quota, though it is difficult to say whether this decision was solely due to the new legislation or whether other factors were involved (Bøhren and Staubo, 2016; Smale, 2013; Terjesen, Aguilera, and Lorenz, 2014). A further factor is that the receptiveness of men towards women who are appointed through quotas may be less than if the women were appointed in the traditional fashion, and problems of in-group and out-group classifications, as highlighted by social categorization theory (Tajfel, 1981) may be exacerbated (Hillman, Shropshire, and Canella, 2007).

The Parker Review (Parker, 2017) examined the issue of diversity and recommended that every board of a FTSE100 organisation should have at least one minority director by 2021. According to Spencer Stuart UK, only 8% of the firms have a minority director. UK citizens from such backgrounds account for just 2% of roles, despite making up 14% of the population (Spencer Stuart UK, 2019).

2.4.5 Employee Representation

In many countries, employee representation on the board is common. The number or proportion of employee representatives on the board varies between different countries, depending on their national legal framework and also according to whether the organisation is state-owned or private, the nature of financing it enjoys, and also in some cases, the number of employees it has (Munkholm, 2018). The type of employee representative permitted to be on the board also varies to some extent. In some countries (e.g. Germany) it is permissible to have an outsider (e.g. an external trade union member), rather than an employee representative. In the Netherlands, the representative must have no connections with the company at all, either as employee or as a trade union figure who negotiates with the company; it must be a person who has a 'special interest or qualification to speak on employee issues to the board' (Munkholm, 2018: 9).

Employee representation on the board differs from employee consultation (Munkholm, 2018). Employee directors are full directors and are not there simply to represent the workforce (Lawrence, 2017). They are there to look at the full range of board issues. Their role, like every other director, is to look after the general interests of the organisation. Similarly, they are also bound by the same terms of confidentiality regarding board information (Sikka et al., 2018).

Though models of employee representation vary, the commitment to employee representatives is clear and is at the heart of a broader stakeholder model of the organisation and highlights a more social rather than economic contract with employees. Having employee representation can also help widen stakeholder engagement and improve board behaviour to ensure a strong decision-making context (ETUI 2017, TUC 2016). Importantly, employee representation can be seen as a key element in combatting short-termism, to which the shareholder model is particularly susceptible (Lawrence, 2017) and in enhancing greater democracy and sense of ownership within organisations.

UK and US companies have long resisted employee representation on the board, citing concerns about inefficiency in decision making and lack of flexibility in responding to changes in the market environment. In section 5, I shall highlight some ideas as to how this perspective may be changing.

2.5 Conclusion

Recently, researchers have developed an algorithm to select directors to the board (Erel, Stern, Tan, and Weisbach, 2018). Running a comparison between effective and ineffective directors regarding monitoring, the study found that the algorithm chose the most effective ones, who turned out to be not part of the friendship network of other directors and who had different backgrounds to the directors on their boards. At the conclusion of the study, the researchers state that 'we use 21st century technology to confirm an observation that dates back over two hundred years: the board selection process leads to directors who are often those nearest at hand and are not necessarily the best choices to serve shareholders' interests.' (Erel et al., 2018: 34).

How the board is composed is a vital ingredient in the dynamics and overall performance of the board. Who sits on the board, their level of skills, knowledge, behaviour and attitudes, their motivation for being a director, and the diversity of thought that exists within the group, will significantly determine how the board behaves and interacts, both internally and also in communication with stakeholders.

I have highlighted some concerns here. The still low levels of diversity in gender and ethnic representation and the worryingly small talent pools for non-executive directors reflect the legacy of old-fashioned approaches to selection. The problem of director demographic similarity remains. It is clear that director demographic similarity encourages deference within the board (Joshi and Knight, 2015). Further it is well-evidenced that if CEOs have strong power over director selection to the board, a weaker board will result over time (Bebchuk and Fried, 2004). The use of nomination committees is an important mechanism to ensure a more balanced approach to the selection of directors. But more needs to be done. One solution is to prioritise diversity. The problem is that research on the connection between board diversity and organisational performance is equivocal. But this is a problem that bedevils all board research. Trying to establish linkages between board variables and outcomes is extremely difficult because of intervening variables that muddy the water. Instead we have to look at arguments of fairness and the reduction of inequality, and the need for greater representation to curtail short-termism. First, the time has come for employee directors to be appointed to boards across public companies. The need for greater perspective and more inclusive decision making would be greatly enhanced by their presence. I explore this more in section 5. Second, commitments to gender and ethnic minority representation must be encouraged further. Though there are positive signs, the progress is still too slow. Greater publicity of success to build further momentum would be of great value, and identification of laggard companies may also serve to sharpen attention. Third, the talent pool must be expanded to include candidates in other spheres, such as not-for-profits, government agencies and the third sector. This idea has been mooted many times but few firms have embraced it, citing the need for industry and general business experience. But this is to downplay the experience of people who have run large departments in non-commercial contexts, or who have strong insights to give from advisory work or research. This addition of greater cognitive diversity may also help solve the problem of directors holding too many appointments (or 'over-boarding'), which the current small talent pool encourages.

Encouraging more diverse boards may lead to a greater appreciation of wider social impact of organisations and so lead to a strengthening of corporate purpose and the social benefits that may arise from it.

3 Dynamics and Process

It is the board that decides the purpose, the social impact, the strategy and operations of the organisation. But academic research and practitioner literature frequently points to the inadequacy of the board in fulfilling its duties.

I mentioned in the introduction that the board is variously claimed to be 'captured' by management, or is merely ceremonial and unengaged, or perhaps even incompetent (e.g. Boivie et al., 2016; Hendry, 2002).

Others would argue that most boards are getting along just fine (Moos and Pecchio, 2012). Much of the bad publicity for boards stems from scandals which are by their nature high profile cases, inevitably complex and multifaceted, and unrepresentative of the vast majority of well-run organisations. Also, the idea that governance reform in board structure and process could eliminate scandals and examples of malfeasance is unrealistic. There will always be examples of bad practice but the vast majority of firms are well governed and current structural arrangements look robust.

This tension is central to corporate governance debates as organisations and regulators and other stakeholders attempt to rebalance the board's possibilities for influence and effectiveness. In section 2 I discussed the issues of board composition, size and structure as key elements of how the board can play its role well or otherwise. In this section I examine the research on the dynamics of the board and highlight what enables or constrains the board in effectively carrying out its roles.

Until recently, boards have been considered as something close to a 'black box', but studies of board dynamics have been increasing (Westphal and Zajac, 2013). Getting inside the board and understanding the processes and interactions that happen there is clearly crucial if we are to understand and improve the contribution and performance of boards. In addition, there is the emergent issue of trust within the boardroom.

Boards can be characterised as 'large, elite, and episodic decision-making groups that face complex tasks pertaining to strategic-issue processing' (Forbes and Milliken, 1999: 492). There is a great deal of research focusing on the nature of workgroups within organisations in general, and some of this work applies strongly to boards of directors. But boards of directors are also atypical of most workgroups for several reasons. First, boards, particularly of larger (and listed) organisations usually include a cadre of independent non-executive directors. The non-executive directors have a limited knowledge of the host firm and also limited time to understand and contribute to it, giving rise to problems of information asymmetry with the executive directors. Second, as I mentioned in section 2, boards have to carry out multiple roles, most notably, the monitoring of senior management and providing advice and counsel to them, and these roles may be in tension with each other (Sundaramurthy and Lewis, 2003). Third, boards meet only infrequently, thus rendering traditional workgroup means of developing dynamics and cohesion problematic.

With these differences in mind, we can start to delve into what makes boards work regarding their dynamics and process. In section 1 I discussed the principal characterisation of the board as an information processing group (Boivie et al., 2016). Central to this idea is the consideration that for a board of directors to work well, it must be 'able to effectively acquire the right information, process it based upon their individual and shared expertise, and then share it as a group with the relevant interested parties,' (Boivie et al., 2016: 324). Boards obviously differ in the extent to which they carry out this information processing role. In this section I shall look at how and why this variation occurs,

I organise the section as follows. First, I discuss the reasons for variation in board involvement across companies. I shall argue this is a factor of board leadership, in particular the Chair, the use of skills, knowledge, behaviour and attitudes within boards, and the norms and practices within the board that may enable or inhibit their use. I will then analyse the elements of board process, including principally the conduct of meetings, and how these elements influence the interaction of directors.

3.1 Variation in Board Involvement

Boards differ greatly in the degree to which they involve themselves in the work of the organisation (Pettigrew and McNulty, 1995). Some operate at high involvement, fully embracing their monitoring and advisory roles, and thereby adding real value to the organisation. At the other end of the continuum, boards are more ceremonial, and act merely as rubber-stampers to the decisions made by the executives. To explore this continuum, we highlight a number of factors that enable or constrain board involvement. I begin with the individual who is deemed to manage the board: the Chair.

3.1.1 Board Leadership; The Role of the Chair

The Chair sets the board's tone and direction, and establishes the performance environment for members of the board (Krause, Semadeni, and Withers, 2016; Useem, 2006). When the board Chair is separate from the CEO, the Chair acts as 'a primary communication channel between the CEO and the rest of the board (Krause et al., 2016: 1991). The relationship that the Chair develops with the CEO is of utmost importance. In our work we have seen the key to this relationship is a negotiated sense of individual and collective responsibilities, an understanding that the Chair role is non-executive and the Chair is not there to be a 'back seat driver'. Further, the Chair should have no executive ambition within the organisation (Roberts and Stiles, 1999).

A strong Chair is aware that 'the board is the collective "boss" of the CEO and that the task of the Chair is to make sure the board provides the goals, resources, rules, and accountability the CEO needs' (Shekshnia, 2018).

The relationship between the two individuals should demonstrate a candid and honest way of working, informed by a common purpose and understanding of the aims of the organisation. This relationship will operate for both the monitoring role of the board, with the Chair offering insight into performance of the firm, and on the CEO themselves, and also for the advisory role, with the Chair giving counsel to the CEO on issues on strategy and change management (Carpenter and Westphal, 2001).

Strong Chairs also prepare for a board meeting effectively, focusing on the contributions that will be made through presentations and discussions and reports, and identifying who will speak when and ensuring that all voices will be heard throughout the meeting (Roberts, 2002).

Effective Chairs meet with the non-executives individually to discuss their concerns and contributions. The Chair is responsible for ensuring that the various elements of the board come together cohesively (Krause et al., 2016).

The degree to which the Chair can develop a safe and productive environment for board discussion and decision-making will crucially determine the effectiveness of the board.

3.1.2 The Use of Human and Social Capital

In section 2, I highlighted the need for boards to have appropriate human and social capital to function well. This will involve both broad-based business knowledge and also firm-specific knowledge, and directors should either possess this knowledge or access it through external contacts and networks (Forbes and Milliken, 1999). However, as is clear from much research on workgroups, possession of knowledge does not entail that the knowledge will be *used* effectively. For a board to be effective, directors must feel motivated to share their knowledge with others in the board and that the knowledge must be combined with others and integrated into the organisation's decision-making. Two issues are particularly important here: effort norms and deference norms.

Effort norms Directors may differ in their judgement about how much effort they should give to expressing their knowledge within the boardroom. Because directors have heavy workloads and so experience time and prioritisation pressures, the degree of attentiveness and contribution to debates within the host organisation may vary widely. These 'effort norms' (Forbes and Milliken, 1999) can develop from an individual's perception of how much attentiveness and participation to bring to the table, to become a group norm, reflecting the shared perception of the group. The same is true in reverse. The board's sense of the level of effort it should invest may influence the effort put forward by new members of the board.

Deference norms In addition to considerations of effort norms, directors may also be subject to norms of deference (Boivie et al., 2016; Westphal and Zajac, 2013). Deference is defined as a 'willingness to yield to another's preferences or opinions as a sign of respect or reverence' (Fragale, Sumanth, Tiedens, and Northcraft, 2012: 374). Deference is a form of politeness (Brown and Levinson, 1987). However, whereas politeness is concerned with 'phrasing things in such a way as to take into consideration the feelings of others' (Brown and Levinson,

1987: 2) deference is more specifically a way to show appeasement and yielding to others. As Boivie et al (2016: 340) argue: 'norms against speaking up in board meetings are especially likely to stifle candid discussion regarding proposals that are considered contrary to the interests of management'. If boards are information processing groups (Boivie et al., 2016) then norms of deference may inhibit the capability of directors to share and integrate information effectively.

Deference can be influenced by a board being too cohesive, which can lead to groupthink. This can be particularly the case when directors are chosen from a similar demographic background (Westphal and Khanna, 2003) (I discussed the similarity hypothesis in section 2). The selection of directors has also been shown to induce norms of reciprocity (Wade, O'Reilly, and Chandratat, 1990; Westphal and Clement, 2008; Westphal et al., 2012), where newly appointed directors feel loyalty to the CEO who agreed to their selection. Breaking this norm can result in sanctions against the director concerned, including social distancing and lack of recommendation for other board appointments (Westphal and Khanna, 2003). Deference is often used as a form of ingratiatory tactic by directors to secure their place on a board and also to win board places at other organisations through referral (Westphal and Stern, 2006), and any behaviour such as voicing a challenging opinion may threaten these aims and so would be avoided.

Given these potential risks in speaking up, directors may be hesitant to voice a divergent view, and may wait until they are convinced that their stance would be supported by others on the board. This may give rise to 'pluralistic ignorance', defined as 'a situation in which virtually all members of a group privately reject group norms, [practices, or policies, or have concerns about them] but believe that virtually all other group members accept them' (Miller, Monin, and Prentice, 2000: 103). The hesitancy to voice an opinion until others do so is a pervasive phenomenon in many social groups (Westphal and Bednar, 2005).

3.1.3 Power and Status

Problems of voice are tied to theories of power and status (Fragale et al., 2012; Westphal and Zajac, 2013). Deference can signal acknowledgement that an individual accepts his or her place within the power and status ordering of the organisation (Fragale et al., 2012). Within boards of directors there is an inherent ambiguity about power and status. Whether there is a rank order within a board is unclear and may vary from board to board. In boards where the hierarchy is clear, deference behaviours indicates acceptance of the status order and that the hierarchy is stable and unlikely to be threatened. Such a context is functional since, in order to get tasks done, individuals must accept that others may have greater expertise or influence. Where the hierarchy is unclear, work on deference among peers, or 'lateral deference' also shows that, as in a hierarchy, deference may well be common, since in such contexts, it may be risky to overestimate one's status in case this may be considered unjustified and so be liable to social sanction (Fragale et al., 2012). Thus, the dynamics of the board depend on the balance of power and status, both formal and informal, between the executive directors and the non-executive directors. Executive power (or the 'managerial hegemony' perspective) particularly focuses on the whether the CEO can 'capture' or silence the non-executive directors. Executive power and a clear and accepted status hierarchy brings with it the ability to control the agenda of the board meeting, the process by which the board is run, and also the selection process for new directors (Cannella and Lubatkin, 1993; Ellstrand, Tihanyi, and Johnson, 2002; Finkelstein and Hambrick, 1996). This will likely reduce the monitoring potential of the board and also the chances of advice giving which may represent a challenge to executive decisions.

3.1.4 Conflict

When contributions are made in the boardroom, there will be differences in judgement between directors concerning the tasks of the board. Because of the uncertainty, complexity and often the novelty of issues that come to the board, disagreements may be inevitable, given that directors will frame issues differently and will also have different views as to the correct responses to the issues at hand. Such differences have been termed 'cognitive conflict' (Forbes and Milliken, 1999: 491). Boards will vary in the extent to which such differences or cognitive conflict is tolerated. For some boards, cognitive conflict may be seen as producing more ideas and greater diversity of thought, thus enhancing the effectiveness of the board. Supporting this is the idea that greater cognitive conflict signals that the board has strong relative power vis a vis the executives.

However, for cognitive conflict to happen, there is need of a culture of trust and respect. Without trust and respect, the basic functions of a group such as challenging questions and candid communications become impossible. A high degree of psychological safety should be present within the boardroom. Psychological safety denotes group members being able to give their views without concern for repercussions (Edmondson, 1999). By developing psychological safety, board members feel encouraged to provide contributions and so enrich discussions and ultimately decision-making.

Cognitive conflict also has strong potential downsides, including cognitive dissonance and negative emotions, (Forbes and Milliken, 1999), and so psychological safety is paramount to ensure the management of such potential outcomes.

3.2 Board Process

In addition to board dynamics, there is also the crucial element of board process. The board meeting and how it is organised is a central mechanism of corporate governance. In this section I outline some of the core aspects of effective board meetings.

3.2.1 Board Agenda Calendar

A board meeting is the responsibility of the Chair (Spencer Stuart UK, 2019). A highly important area for framing the meeting is the board agenda calendar. The development of the agenda calendar is usually decided between the Chair and the CEO. Typically, an annual schedule of issues to be discussed at the board is drawn up. Similar schedules may be put in place for the board committees. Overall, such schedules are useful for making sure that the key business themes facing the organisation are dealt with appropriately and that the participation of board members is encouraged.

In addition to the planning of the agenda calendar, directors should be invited to add items to the agenda at any time.

A frequent complaint voiced by directors in board process research is the time spent in meeting on largely operational matters rather than on the high levels issues that should characterise board endeavour. Further, the agenda should highlight forward-looking activities rather than overly focus on performance (McKinsey, 2016).

3.2.2 Matters Reserved for the Board

Many companies specify the matters that should come before the board for decision (Useem, 2006). This specification – called 'reserved powers' or 'delegation of authority' – ensures a clear demarcation between the board and management and helps to build the board calendar and set of priorities. The list may also extend to highlighting the issues to be dealt with at board committee level also in so called 'committee charters'.

3.2.3 Meeting Papers

Board agendas will usually feature a considerable range of themes. Because directors, and in particular the non-executives, are very busy, board papers need to be precise and succinct (Useem, 2006). The agenda will generally be organised in priority order, with the more important items coming at the beginning. Clear and consistent formatting of papers, and of the board pack overall, is also important, in order for directors to read information as efficiently as possible.

The board papers need to be sent out well in advance – at least one week before the meeting – to give enough time for directors to read and absorb the information.

3.2.4 Meeting Frequency

The frequency with which boards meet may also determine the effectiveness of the board process. For most boards of large companies, there are seven or more board meetings a year, with most boards meeting for three to five hours (Spencer Stuart UK, 2019). Boards of dispersed international organisations may meet less frequently but for longer, due to the logistical issues involved. Naturally, meetings may increase in frequency as events emerge to challenge organisations.

3.2.5 The Non-Executive Directors' Meeting

In unitary board jurisdictions, some companies hold meetings for only the Chair and the non-executive directors, to enable a good, detailed discussion without the executive team present. In the UK, the Combined Code also recommends that there should be an annual meeting of the non-executives without the Chair present, to be hosted by the senior independent director.

3.3 Conclusion

Board research has focused largely on functions or roles within boards of directors (Daily, Dalton, and Canella, 2003; Demb and Neubauer, 1992) and on identifying the significant aspects of board roles, primarily two (i) monitoring the behaviour of managers in the organisation and (ii) the provision of advice and resources. It is clear however there is variation in the enactment of these two roles.

The structural elements of boards, including their composition and independence, provide a context within which directors can operate and be effective. But they do not account for how particular relationships and dynamics within these structures will play out. There are a number of social psychological forces within the board that may inhibit directors from expressing independence of judgement and limit use of expertise.

Stemming from our discussion in section 2, an issue affecting the independence of board members is the demographic similarity of independent non-executive directors. The small talent pool for independent non-executive directors and the need to widen the market for them has been identified (see, for example, Higgs, 2002). The similarity of background and view may have advantages in terms of expertise but may limit independence of mind (Roberts et al., 2005). In addition, there are norms of reciprocity among directors who also serve as independent directors on other boards which may hinder the performance of independent oversight (Westphal and Zajac, 2013).

Creating a workable dynamic within the boardroom is dependent on the conduct of directors and how relationships are developed that embrace the need for cohesion and deference at times, but also allow for challenge and review. The work of the Chair in achieving this balance is critical. For a board to work well, it must be able to process information effectively and make decisions appropriately. Having the resources to carry out the roles (for example, being given enough information from the company to make accurate judgements, and having access to key sources of professional guidance) are highly important.

The way in which board process is organised will also have a significant effect on how the board operates as a group. How the board meeting is run, the agenda, papers, timing, and frequency of meetings, will all affect how information is introduced and processed within the board.

Together, both board dynamics and board process create the conditions for constructive contribution and challenging discussion on purpose, strategy, risks, and operations of the organisation (Pye and Pettigrew, 2005; Roberts et al., 2005; Westphal and Zajac, 2013). As the quality of information processing increases within the board, the transparency of decision-making will also increase, and the explainability and justification of the board's actions will be enhanced.

Being able to give a good account of its actions is a prime responsibility for boards. Boards are held to account by shareholders and stakeholders for the performance of the organisation and also for the performance of the board itself. In the next section, I turn to this issue specifically.

4 Board Accountability

We have seen that the nature of board engagement can vary, depending on a number of factors, including board composition, the presence and use of human and social capital of directors, their effort norms, the norms of deference, the balance of power and status between the executives and the non-executives, and the quality of the board processes such as the meeting preparation, facilitation, and focus.

We have also seen that the roles of the board involve two main aspects: monitoring and advice giving. For boards to be effective they have to embrace both roles. This is not straightforward since to deliver on the monitoring role, non-executive directors are required to maintain a distance from executives and to oversee them, whereas with advice giving, there is a need to build close relationships with executives to ensure trust and openness.

This tension has tended to provoke a polarised sense of director effectiveness, and fuelled a sense that directors have to 'wear two hats' (Ezzamel and Watson, 1997) to ensure board effectiveness, cognitively switching regularly between the two major roles. One of the problems of this separation is that it may encourage a dualism perspective of non-executive directors as being either monitors or supporters. Work in paradox theory adopts a duality view, arguing that non-executive directors have to embrace both behaviours. For example, Sundaramurthy and Lewis (2003) theorised that both control and collaboration are part of the director's role, and that either element – control or collaboration – should not be emphasised at the expense of the other, or else this may prompt either distrust if there is too much control, or capture, if there is too much collaboration. In empirical work on accountability in the board (Roberts et al., 2005), non-executive directors see their role as engaging in dialogue with executives in relation to both current monitoring and advice-giving. For example:

> *'describing the work of the non-executive in terms of creating accountability brings us much closer to the conduct and practices – questioning, probing, challenging, inter alia through which they can be effective. Rather than an awkward switching between control and collaboration, skillful accountability combines elements of both'* (Roberts et al., 2005: s18).

Focusing just on structural elements in governance and boards will therefore only give a very partial view of board endeavour and may indeed provide a false sense of security for stakeholders, who may find reassurance that with the right structures in place, the organisation is being effectively run (Roberts, 2009). Accountability is much more determined by the behavioural dynamics within the board and the set of relationships that exist between board members (Huse, 2007). The problem for stakeholders is that they cannot see the nature of interaction between board members, and so judging whether a board is interacting well and ensuring accountability is problematic from this point of view. It is to this problem that I turn in the current section.

The section is structured as follows. First, I look at some of the principal ways in which board performance and accountability are conceptualised. The perspective of investors will be outlined, and then I will examine accountability from the point of view of delivering social purpose. I will then turn to other core measures of board performance, including innovation and tone from the top.

I conclude by examining board performance regarding the board itself, and the key measure of cohesion.

4.1 Boards, Accountability and Performance

Boards are at the heart of organisational performance. They are lauded when things go well, and vilified in the wake of organisational underperformance and scandal. According to most views of governance, the shareholders of the organisation delegate the responsibility to the board of directors to oversee management and ensure that the interests of the company are prioritised. The board then is accountable for how it bears this responsibility (Keay and Loughrey, 2015; Power, 1997). So how is accountability manifested? This question, which has long been a subject of both academic and practitioner debate, is complex, primarily for three reasons. First, the definition of what accountability means, and what are the measures being used to assess it, are far from straightforward issues. There is a multiplicity of approaches to judge the accountability of a board and depending on the measure, the role of the board may be more or less opaque in influencing outcomes. Second, accountability for whom? Boards have responsibilities to shareholders and a range of stakeholders, whose demands on the organisation may be in conflict, so judgements of accountability will depend on which lens is being used to assess outcomes. Third, accountability over what timescale? For some stakeholders, short-term delivery on say profitability, and/or share price, may be the most important criterion whereas for others, a long-term approach to value creation, investing in research and development, and building a sustainable future for the organisation, would be more appropriate.

These difficulties stem in part from the specification of directors' duties. The UK Companies Act (2006; Section 172) states that directors have 'duty to promote the success of the company.' This is glossed further as follows: 'A director of a company must act in the way he (sic) considers, in good faith, would be most likely to promote the success of the company for the benefit of its members as a whole' and in doing so 'have regard to' a series of factors relating to the need to consider the long term implications of decisions and to foster good relationships with the company's stakeholders.

This reflects an enlightened shareholder value perspective, and suggests that companies have a legal duty to conduct business in a way that accounts for sustainable growth and success and takes into account the impact of its activities on stakeholders (Barker, 2013; Keay and Loughery, 2015). The term 'have regard to' is open to a large degree of interpretation. For this reason, some commentators believe that the provision should be reformed to place shareholders and stakeholders on an equal footing, and not, as now, have shareholders placed above stakeholders (Lawrence, 2017; Sikka et al., 2018). The argument here is that shareholders remain primary, and stakeholders are to be taking into account only to the point of where they go against what would be perceived to conflict with the 'success' of the company.

Others believe that the section has considerable force, for example: 'notwithstanding the unlikelihood of enforcement action arising from breach of any of its particular doctrinal components, section 172 undeniably retains considerable 'soft' behavioural influence as a salient and authoritative public statement of the proper corporate objective in the UK' (Moore, 2016: 7). Objections to putting stakeholders on the same level as shareholders rest to a large degree on the perceived difficulties in directors balancing the often-competing interests of different stakeholders, and so losing the focus for the company provided by the enlightened shareholder approach. But it could be argued that most large companies are already balancing stakeholders in this way in their normal practice (Moore, 2016).

In the US shareholder primacy is the norm, (Rhee, 2017), with its development traced to the Chicago School of economists in the 1970s notably Milton Friedman, who argued that the only 'social responsibility of business is to increase its profits' (Posner, 2019). But as mentioned in section 1, the Business Roundtable statement on the Purpose of a Corporation (2019) and the proposed Accountable Capitalism Act show that greater focus on stakeholders may be the way to produce greater prosperity for the US overall. I shall say more about this in section 5, when we consider possible changes to the current way of organising boards. But one thing common to both approaches is that success will generally mean an increase in value.

For most organisations a key measure of performance will be the overall financial performance of the organisation. A great deal of research has been carried out with the aim of linking board attributes to financial performance. From the research literature, however, it is clear that board structural characteristics, particularly on composition, and on independence seem to have no link with firm performance (e.g., Bhagat et al., 2008; Dalton et al., 1998). In addition, meta-analyses show no evidence of systematic relationships between board composition and corporate financial performance (Bhagat et al., 2008; Dalton et al., 2008; Daily et al., 2003; Dalton et al., 1998; Fogel and Grier, 2007; Rhoades et al., 2000; Wagner, Steimpert, and Fubara, 1998)

The attempt to link board composition variables to other forms of performance, such as innovation, and creativity, and environmental care, have also produced equivocal results (Klarner, Probst, and Useem, 2019). This is not to say of course that board composition or structural governance elements are not important in organisational performance. But at present, the number of intervening variables that may influence the relationship remain under-researched (Daily et al., 2003; Hermalin and Weisbach, 2003)

We know from section 2 that board composition and governance structure are important to the effective running of organisations for the legitimacy and confidence they bring for investors and stakeholders, and also to ensure that good board dynamics can be realised. But they themselves are not sufficient to deliver performance. Equally important, as we saw in section 3, are the dynamics and process that the board develops, encompassing such issues as how well does the board attend to its duties; what time and energy is devoted to particular issues; how diligent and knowledgeable are directors in their monitoring and advisory roles? As we have seen, the list of issues for the attention of directors is considerable, ranging across such elements as strategy, monitoring, risk, innovation, culture, and talent. For boards to deliver performance they have to attend to this myriad of tasks.

A recent McKinsey survey (2014) helps to shed some light on this. Drawing on responses from 770 directors of public and private and non-profit organisations across industries around the world, the study suggests that boards demonstrating moderate performance did the 'basics' of ensuring compliance, reviewing financial reports, and so on. But those judged to have a higher impact engaged in these more intensely and also were committed to 'meta'-practices – deliberating on the processes they used and trying to make them better.

These differences in attention and intensity are therefore very important in how board performance is enacted. I begin to explore these issues first by looking at board task performance and relate this to major organisational performance outcomes, comprising financial performance, strategic performance, and innovation. I shall then turn to the issue of board cohesion and examine the way performance is perceived and assessed in this area.

4.2 Judgements about Board Task Performance

How is board performance judged? What are the expectations of boards and what enables or derails high performance from them? I noted earlier that academic research does not tell us much about the board's impact directly on firm performance. But what is clear from looking at the public statements of major stakeholder groups is that financial performance and strategic direction are central criteria used to judge board performance. One way to look at this is to examine the example of the most visible assessors of board performance – active investors – who target companies and boards they perceive to be underperforming.

Activist campaigns targeted at companies and their boards reached an all-time record in 2019, with 25 campaigns launched at a cost of $7.35bn (£5.72bn) on shares (FT, 2019). A recent survey by Korn Ferry (2017) highlighted a number of major concerns activist investors have with boards of directors generally:

Value of assets is not being realised. A major reason for activist attention is the perception that the value of some assets is not being realised. The board is perceived to be 'asleep at the wheel' or lacking capability to improve the performance of the asset. For example, the Barclays Bank board is under pressure from active investor Edward Bramson to scale back the investment banking arm of the bank on the perception that it is contributing to a drain on resources and management attention and causing the share price of the firm to suffer (BBC, 2019).

The whole company is worth less than the sum of the parts. Companies are frequently seen as having assets which would realise more value if they were hived off. For example, activist fund Elliott Advisors pressured the Whitbread board into hiving off the Costa Coffee business from the Premier Inn hotel business to realise more value for the firm, arguing the break up could realise £3.2bn of value (Kollewe, 2018).

Share price is lagging. Investors will look to a low share price as an indicator that the board is not operating optimally. A number of firms in the UK have been highlighted by investors as targets for activism for this reason, including Centrica, Kingfisher, and Next (Martin, 2019).

Lack of strategic direction. Boards can be a source of inertia (Hoppman, Naegele, and Girod, 2019). The literature on strategic change and vision has long studied the source of organisational inertia and how firms can adapt to changes in their environment (Romanelli and Tushman, 1994). Boards are required to overcome strategic inertia and drive the organisation forward. For example, in September 2019 Elliott Management took a $3.2 billion stake in AT&T, and highlighted the need for increased strategic focus, particularly questioning the strategic merit of the merger with Time Warner and other non-core diversification.

Too much cash on the balance sheet. Activist investors tend to object to large amounts of cash sitting on the balance sheet. For example, famously ValueAct Capital, an activist firm, won a Microsoft board seat in 2013 by criticising the company's huge cash balance of $77 billion, double that of its peers.

Uncompetitive versus rivals. A company that performs below a competitive benchmark or against its rivals and with no clear plan or evidence that it has found a way to get better, will find its board the subject of investor scrutiny. For example, US tech firm Verint was targeted by major shareholder Neuberger Berman in February 2019 due to the concerns about declining cash flows and the company lagging behind its peers. Neuberger Berman wanted to get three new directors on the board (which failed) and also to force the firm to adopt return on invested capital as a measure of performance, to show firm performance more accurately, rather than maintain its reliance on non-GAAP (generally accepted accounting principles) metrics that showed the company as leading in the industry (Trainer, 2019).

High pay not linked to performance. Activist investors become very exercised by firms where large pay awards for executives do not reflect the achievement of stated strategic and operational goals (Larcker and Tryan, 2016). Executive pay is often subject to camouflage and obfuscation (Bebchuk and Fried, 2004). In 2002 in the UK and 2007 in the US, advisory votes for shareholders on executive pay came into force (Hodgson, 2009), but despite the ability for shareholders to vote on executive pay, most shareholders approve pay as usual for CEOs and executives. Activist investors continue to highlight non-performance-related remuneration as a clear sign of a lack of management accountability and worthy of direct intervention.

Board performance will be scrutinised on these dimensions by activist investors and improvements will be sought if one or several elements are deemed to be lacking.

4.3 Risk and Performance

The UK Corporate Governance Code (FCA, 2018: principle O) states that 'The board should establish procedures to manage risk, oversee the internal control framework, and determine the nature and extent of the principal risks the company is willing to take in order to achieve its long-term strategic objectives.' Similar statements are present in a number of jurisdictions, and the board's oversight of risk, in strategic, financial, operational or compliance areas, is now a major feature of board work and provides an important measure of board performance.

Boards are focused on risk oversight rather than risk management (Gupta and Leech, 2017) with a clear aim to determine that the risk policies and process set down by management are appropriate to the organisational strategy and environmental context. As Lipton (2015: para. 2) states:

> The board should be aware of the type and magnitude of the company's principal risks and should require that the CEO and the senior executives are fully engaged in risk management. Through its oversight role, the board can send a message to management and employees that comprehensive risk

management is not an impediment to the conduct of business nor a mere
supplement to a firm's overall compliance program. Instead, it is an integral
component of strategy, culture and business operations.

Most organisations have an enterprise risk management framework which details particular risk categories to be reviewed and managed. This board responsibility has in some cases been allocated to a board committee, usually the audit committee, and more organisations now have dedicated risk committees as part of their governance structure. This has generated a lot of controversy. The regulatory requirements differ. On the New York Stock Exchange, risk oversight is delegated to the audit committee whereas for other jurisdictions, it is a board level responsibility. For financial institutions, often a separate risk committee is required. Recent work by Ittner and Keutsch (2015) on 297 publicly-traded firms worldwide showed that boards with a separate risk committee had lower board and management alignment on risk management objectives, suggesting the need to ensure the board as a whole should deal with risk, and not delegate the issue to a sub-committee.

So, while board committees may oversee specific risks, the whole board must be engaged in reviewing all risks. For this reason, boards need to have directors with industry knowledge and also directors with diverse backgrounds to bring diversity of thought and perspective to examining the risks facing the organisation and also to look at the risk/reward balance when considering innovation activities.

Dodd-Frank requires at least one risk management expert on the risk committee of major financial firms (Lipton, Niles, and Miller, 2018). Many firms have a chief risk officer who has a seat on the board. Fundamentally, the governance of risk management requires the appropriate mix of board members with appropriate expertise.

4.4 Boards and Innovation

Innovation is considered essential to a firm's growth and sustainability (Wu, 2008). According to the National Association of Corporate Directors (NACD)'s 2017–18 Public Company Governance Survey, industry disruption and business model innovation are two of the top trends corporate directors anticipate will impact their companies. Innovation is also now a top 5 business priority of CEOs globally, and 'creating an innovation culture' is the leading item for innovation itself (NACD, 2018).

However, just what is the board's role in innovation? Innovation is a broad term and each organisation may attach a different meaning to it. But generally speaking, innovation can be defined as 'the adoption of a new idea, whether a new product, process, service, technology, or practice' (Klarner et al., 2019: 2).

The board's role in innovation has two major aspects. First, board directors themselves may be the focus of innovation by bringing new knowledge and capabilities to the organisation and thereby providing different perspectives that can increase the potential for innovation. Second, board directors can set the parameters for innovation within the organisation through developing the norms for innovative behaviour. Let us take each in turn.

For the first aspect, I have discussed the resource dependence approach and the role non-executive directors play in bringing new knowledge to the organisation and drawing on expert networks to deliver new resources (Hillman, Canella, and Paetzold, 2000; Kim and Canella, 2008). In addition, non-executives may promote a longer-term view than executives, since executives prefer more immediate pay-offs in investments rather than riskier longer-term investments (Baysinger et al., 1991; Fama and Jensen, 1983). But a number of studies have also pointed to a dysfunctional effect of non-executive directors on the board concerning innovation. The argument is that executives know most about the firm and its products and processes and so decisions about changing these will be based on better knowledge and have more likelihood of success than if the board is composed predominantly by non-executive directors (Baysinger et al.,1991; Hoskisson et al., 2002).

Second, the board can set the parameters for innovation within the organisation. By taking a long-term view towards strategic planning, examining both strong and weak environmental signals, and ensuring appropriate analysis of changing and disruptive conditions, the board can provide the conditions in which the organisation can adapt appropriately to changing circumstances and develop innovative approaches to sustain the organisation. Boards can also support the context for innovation by establishing an appropriate culture for innovation. This would involve working with management to set a performance framework for innovation, including developing innovation goals and an aligned reward structure for innovation practice. Innovation should also be a regular feature on the board agenda, and feature strongly at strategy away days. Discussions here would review the organisation's innovation strategy, and also include the progress of major innovation projects. Also, a number of boards include the organisation's innovation risk within their regular risk oversight assessment. As Deschamps (2010: para. 8) argues:

> *Boards usually devote a significant amount of time to risk assessment and reduction. But their focus tends to be on financial, environmental, regulatory and geopolitical risk. Innovation risk may be underestimated, except in the*

case of large projects involving huge investments and new technologies. But internal innovation risk is not limited to new project and technology uncertainties. It can be linked to the loss of critical staff, for example. Innovation risk can also be purely external. Will competitors introduce a new disruptive technology that will make our products and processes obsolete? Will new entrants invade our market space through different, more effective business models? Will our customers expect new solutions that we have not thought about?

As always, the board has to oversee the difficult tension between ensuring the day-to-day business is secure and delivering value, while at the same time putting in place structures that will provide a healthy innovation approach to long-term effectiveness of the organisation.

Using metrics to assess the innovation performance is not straightforward, as each organisation will have different goals and risk profiles. A survey of 365 corporate directors on the issue of disruptive technology (Klemash, Lee, and Pederson, 2019) identified the most common indicators used by boards. They found that boards balanced their oversight on three areas: new markets, new products and solutions, and efficiencies within their existing business model. The survey showed revenue from new products and services was the leading metric, with resources allocated to new offerings and innovation return on investment also widely used.

4.5 Purpose and the Tone at the Top

We began the Element by highlighting the growing emphasis on boards determining corporate purpose and the social benefits that will result from it. Performance here will be judged on how boards are putting in place strategies to deliver long-term value creation. Further, the board has to demonstrate that it is overseeing effectively the risks associated with, and systems needed for, the delivery of the long-term plan. The commitments made by the corporate purpose regarding social engagement can also be assessed on whether a positive impact is being made.

With the corporate purpose comes the need to develop a culture of trust and integrity and ethicality (Lipton, 2019). In setting the appropriate 'tone at the top' the board has to demonstrate its commitment to a set of norms that will define the culture of the organisation. These norms would revolve around core values such as fairness and openness, transparency, accountability and performance, integrity and ethical standards (Lipton, 2015). The communication of these norms through the organisation is paramount and so too the way in which directors and senior members of the organisation demonstrate these behaviours within and outside the organisation. What the board of directors emphasises and pays attention to, what are the issues it acts on, and what are the omissions it allows, all provide signals to members of the organisation about the appropriate way to behave. They also provide signals to stakeholders about the performance of the board.

This prompts the question – by what norms or standards of behaviour do directors conduct themselves? This will be noticed by the organisation and its stakeholders and will have a strong effect on the culture overall. A good example concerns McDonalds and the dismissal of their CEO Steve Easterbrook in November 2019. Easterbrook had admitted that he had a romantic relationship with an employee, which is against company policy. Though Easterbrook was widely credited for transforming the company since he became CEO in 2015, nevertheless the company adopted a zero-tolerance policy regarding one of its long-standing policies.

Naturally, the make-up and the dynamics of the board itself will also send a powerful message to the organisation and its stakeholders. For example, does the board's composition reflect values of diversity and inclusion and contain human capital that will allow it to be ethical and sustainable? The way a board makes decisions – whether it does so in the spirit of engagement and consensus building or whether it is achieved through power and factionalism and political behaviour – will also send clear messages to stakeholders (Thuraisingham, 2019). There is a famous phrase in leadership theory which is that leaders are 'always on'. In other words, every move and utterance of directors is being weighed and interpreted by others within and outside the organisation. So, consistency of message and appropriateness of behaviour consonant with the values and norms of the organisation are paramount.

4.6 Board and Governance Practice: Cohesion

A major indicator of performance is whether the board's own performance in meeting key governance criteria are met. For listed companies, this is assessed by the review of board performance annually. The UK Corporate Code (FRC, 2018: provision 21) states:

'There should be a formal and rigorous annual evaluation of the performance of the board, its committees, the chair and individual directors'.

The evaluation process is recommended to cover the following aspects (FRC, 2018a: 29, section 113):

- the mix of skills, experience and knowledge on the board, in the context of developing and delivering the strategy, the challenges and opportunities, and the principal risks facing the company;

- clarity of, and leadership given to, the purpose, direction and values of the company;
- succession and development plans;
- how the board works together as a unit, and the tone set by the chair and the chief executive;
- key board relationships, particularly chair/chief executive, chair/senior independent director, chair/company secretary and executive/non-executive directors;
- effectiveness of individual directors;
- clarity of the senior independent director's role;
- effectiveness of board committees, and how they are connected with the main board;
- quality of the general information provided on the company and its performance;
- quality and timing of papers and presentations to the board;
- quality of discussions around individual proposals and time allowed;
- process the chair uses to ensure sufficient debate for major decisions or contentious issues;
- effectiveness of the company secretary/secretariat;
- clarity of the decision-making processes and authorities, possibly drawing on key decisions made over the year;
- processes for identifying and reviewing risks; and
- how the board communicates with, and listens and responds to, shareholders and other key stakeholders.

This broad set of issues will have a different profile for each board and so a bespoke approach to evaluation is necessary (FRC, 2018a) The regulatory requirements generally stress evaluation of the board as a whole. As indicated by the list above, there is a set of structure-based items, to assess how the board measures up against accepted standards of governance such as the Combined Code or other regulatory recommendations. There is also a list of task-based items which examine how well the board is doing in carrying out its responsibilities, such as its work in strategy, risk, monitoring, accountability, and communication, among others. A further set of items concerns the board's cohesion as a group, looking at issues of group dynamics and the quality of interaction between directors. These evaluation questions are directed to the board as a whole.

There are a lot of tools used to measure board performance, but only a few which have been subject to empirical validation (Nicholson, Kiel, and Tunny,

2012). These include the Governance Self-Assessment Checklist (GSAC) (Gill, Flynn, and Reissing, 2005), the Board Self-Assessment Questionnaire (BSAQ) (Holland, 1991); and Nicholson and Newton's (2010) Board Roles. It is difficult to assess the quality of these models based on the small samples used, problems with construct validity, and wide variation between raters (Nicholson et al., 2012).

In addition to the board's overall performance evaluation, assessing the performance of individual directors may also be in place. Typically, this will involve two aspects, an individual self-evaluation and a peer evaluation. The self-evaluation encourages a reflective sense of the director's own performance and to look for ways in which they can develop their contribution. The peer evaluation asks board members to comment (either anonymously or not) on colleagues and to give candid and constructive feedback. This can take place either through interviews or through questionnaires (Klemash. Doyle and Smith, 2018).

Responsibility for conducting the evaluation of the board rests most often with the Chair (FCA, 2018). There is recognition by commentators and regulators that this may generate a less than objective process, and so it is now common for evaluation conducted by an internal member to be supplemented by one conducted by an external assessor periodically. In the UK, the advice is that a review conducted by an external agent should take place every three years (Financial Reporting Council, 2018). Other jurisdictions have similar requirements (Nicholson et al., 2012).

There have always been concerns that the board evaluation process results in a ceremonial box-ticking exercise that preserves the status quo. With more and more scrutiny of boards and their performance, it is ever more important to have an annual health check of both task performance and team functioning to assess points of improvement.

4.7 Conclusion

Assessing the performance of boards is difficult. Boards are often characterised as 'black boxes' where the dynamics and the process of decision-making and monitoring are opaque. Boards are operating in rarefied conditions, with uncertainty, with a great deal of responsibility, and subject to intense scrutiny. In such contexts, the human side of boards must be remembered. Directors are people too, and they have the full range of emotions and intuitions and cognitive biases that can influence the decision-making process and, under pressure, give less than optimal outcomes. To put it in the language of agency theory, the major problem facing principals is often not that the agent is self-seeking and opportunistic, but rather can suffer from gaps in emotional competence or is prone to lapses of judgement (Hendry, 2002). This thought about agency theory suggests another, which is that for accountability of the board to be delivered under the context of shareholder primacy, there can be a preoccupation with the performance of the firm in light of relatively short-term investment horizons, which can lead to an organisational defensiveness or even evasiveness. But if organisations are more than just economic entities, but fully social ones, then accountability also becomes socially significant (Roberts, 2009). The interdependency between the firms and its stakeholders needs greater consideration. Boards, with all the bounded rationality I have hinted at, are all too often put in the position of defending a series of performance metrics that satisfy shareholders, and so are concerned with protecting a positive reputation but with little thought to its conduct or the effects on others (Roberts, 2009). For example, the demands of activist investors with which I began the section can be helpful in disciplining tired or complacent boards and companies. But too often, activist investors can focus too much on short-term gains and in so doing destroy value for the firm and for society, A good example is Nelson Peltz's Trian Fund investment in DuPont in 2017, and their demands for DuPont to reduce costs by $4bn or be subject to Trian taking full control, with the incumbent management having no control. DuPont acquiesced and made large cuts to research and development expenditure and laid off 5,000 employees, 10% of the workforce (Guarino, 2017). Boards need to attend to financial performance naturally, but accountability is wider than this. Boards cannot afford to downplay risks on ESG concerns, or from technological disruption, or from lack of innovation. The risks from inside the firm, particularly the tone from the top and culture, are also of high importance. For full accountability the board has to look forward, to examine the changing market and environmental landscape and anticipate future risks. The lessons of the financial crisis of 2008 and the coronavirus of 2020 suggest that accountability has to be viewed systemically, and the range of interdependencies with stakeholders have to be fully recognised.

5 Renewing Boards of Directors

The board of directors is an enduring structure in corporate governance. The basic elements of board composition and structure, focusing primarily on the need for independent oversight, advice-giving and providing accountability to stakeholders, have been institutionalised. I have discussed some of the major issues that still affect how the board does its work: the presence and use of human and social capital, the extent of information asymmetry between executives and non-executives, the high demands on non-executive directors' time, the complexity of issues boards face. These continuing themes create further space for reform.

In this final section I shall examine some core proposals for ways to rethink boards. I shall start with the most radical proposal: the replacement of the traditional corporate governance approach with the private equity model. I shall then look at the possibility of reducing directors' independence to shareholders, and the placing of employee representatives on the board. I shall address the calls to reform directors' duties before closing with highlighting new perspectives on board culture and how boards may have to operate differently in an increasingly disruptive environment.

5.1 Rethinking the Corporate Board: The Private Equity Approach

A clear way to deal with the inherent structural problems of boards is, for some, to do away with the current structure and replace it. But what should corporate boards be replaced with? One attempt to put forward an alternative was made by Michael Jensen, famous as one of the leading authors of agency theory. Jensen's idea was that the model of private equity (PE) boards should be universal. Jensen's view is that PE allows the value lost to agency costs to be captured by the firm (Jensen, 1989).

PE boards tend to be populated by owners or their representatives. They tend to share the same level of expectation on risk return. They are also normally in agreement about the timetable for their investment. They will have significant equity (and/or debt) invested and will give full attention to the strategy of the firm. Thus, the directors of PE boards tend to be generally largely homogenous. The board size will be typically small, have much greater focus, and much greater motivation to deliver performance (Jensen, 1989).

This view has been taken up most recently by Ronald Gilson and Jeffrey Gordon (2019), with their concept of 'Board 3.0'. They describe the need to develop a model of 'thickly informed, well-resourced, and highly motivated directors who could credibly monitor managerial strategy and operational skill' (2019: 352). They cite the example of private equity boards 'in which the high-powered incentives of the PE sponsor have produced a different mode of board and director engagement that seems associated with high value creation,' (2019: 352). Their view is that the current corporate board model comprises 'thinly informed, under-resourced, and boundedly motivated directors' (2019: 352).

The adoption of a PE approach would alleviate the problem of board monitoring, and solve the inherent structural weaknesses in traditional board working. For this model to work in a public company, there would, in their view, continue to be a mix of executive and independent directors but also a new set of 'empowered directors':

> *Board 3.0, on our conception, is a board that contains a mix of directors on the current Board 2.0 model and "empowered" directors ("3.0 directors") who would specifically be charged with monitoring the strategy and operational performance of the management team. The 2.0 directors would serve, as now, on compliance-focused committees and otherwise take on the board's responsibilities, especially serving on "special committees" as necessary. The 3.0 directors would serve on an additional committee, the "Strategy Review Committee." Those directors would be supported by an internal "strategic analysis office" that would provide back-up support for a 3.0 director's engagement with the management team.* (Gilson and Gordon, 2019: 360).

The PE model is indeed instructive and provides a clear route to reforming traditionally structured boards. Since Jensen wrote the initial article in 1989 there is some support for his view that the days of listed corporation are numbered. In the US, in 1989, there were 5,000 publicly listed companies, now this figure is at 3,000 (Morris and Phalippou, 2020). In the UK, the number of listed companies has also seen a falling trend, for example in the period from 2015 to 2020, there has been a drop from 2,429 to 2,024. Some of this may be due to mergers, and share buybacks and some of the problems associated with recent IPOs (e.g. WeWork, Aston Martin, Funding Circle) may have put off many from this route to public status. Undoubtedly however, the regulatory burden, the demands for increased reporting and the extra scrutiny of performance of having listed status for many is too burdensome. The number of firms in the US which are PE-backed has risen from 4,000 in 2006 to 8,000 in 2017 (McKinsey, 2019), while in the UK, there is also a rising trend with currently 1,335 firms with PE-funding (BVCA, 2018). In addition, qualitative evidence suggests that directors who have been members of boards under both corporate and PE governance attest that PE boards are significantly more effective than their publicly-listed counterparts (Achyara, Kehoe, and Reyner, 2008).

Does this really support the claim that private equity is a better way to govern the firm? There may be a number of problems with this idea. According to Magnusson (2018) the compensation arrangements for the PE sponsors means that they are incentivised to take excessive risk, since they receive much of the profits from their investments but are to a large extent protected from losses, thus creating a moral hazard. In addition, investors other than those who are limited partners experience significant disadvantages, including unequal access to information, fewer governance rights, and lack of clear opportunities to offload their equity interests in the fund (Magnusson, 2018).

Further, research suggests that CEO control of the private equity board is strong, which may result in over-commitment to a CEO when performance suffers, negating a vital role of the board which is to evaluate and sometimes oust a CEO (O'Brien, 2008).

The most common criticism of private equity is that it fosters short-termism. While private equity can provide a context that promotes long-term decision-making, and can, in a certain light, resemble the stewardship model of governance (Davis et al., 1997; Kay 2012) many PE firms are looking towards maximising returns before exit. As Houlder and Nandkishore (2016: 4) argue 'the weakness of the classic private equity model is the inherent challenge of the exit: It is hard to look strategically beyond the typical three-year exit plan and likely departure of the top management team.'

The PE approach has the merit of placing the spotlight on directors' knowledge and motivation and on what is required to make a significant contribution. However, it introduces moral hazard, unequal treatment of investors and can encourage short-termism.

5.2 Rethinking Directors: Reducing Independence to Shareholders

The thoughts about the value of independent directors inherent in the private equity model suggest that independence is overrated. Other commentators also look at the issue of director independence but look to strengthen rather than weaken it. Insisting on greater director independence does not solve the issues with the board, since it still leaves us with problems of information asymmetry and managerial power. But one emerging view is that while director independence should be preserved, director independence from shareholders should be reduced. As Bebchuk and Fried (2010: 11) argue:

> *The appointment of directors should substantially depend on shareholders, not only in theory but in practice. Such dependence would give directors better incentives to serve shareholder interests. Making directors dependent on shareholders could counter some of the factors that incline directors to pursue their own interests or those of executives rather than those of shareholders.*

According to Bebchuk and Fried (2010) shareholders should be afforded greater powers to remove directors through the elimination of staggered boards. In a staggered board, approximately one-third of directors are elected each year, with the result that for dissatisfied shareholders to replace the majority of directors, they would have to win in two annual elections. They further argue for the right of shareholders to place director candidates on the corporate ballot.

These recommendations are important and would increase the level of accountability within the board. Another area for greater shareholder accountability is dual class shares. Organisations that have a dual class share structure split the shares between A class and B class, with the B class shares having greater voting rights that the A shares. The intention of such a structure is to insulate a group of shareholders, usually the family or the founders, against the threat of takeover or other market discipline, such as activist investors. Such share structures have gained increased interest due to their prevalence within the technology and the media and entertainment sectors, with companies such as Alphabet, Apple, Alibaba, Facebook, We Work among others, using them. For some firms, the voting power of the B-class shares is afforded ten times that of the A-class (e.g. Alphabet) for others, it is thirty times the power (e.g. Facebook), and variations thereof. In some cases, there is a class of shares which has no voting rights (e.g. Alphabet's class C stock). By protecting a particular group of shareholders, it is argued, these firms are able to operate with a long-term perspective, invest in research and development, and ensure that the energy and commitment of the founders is not dissipated by over-concern about possible battles with other investors or acquisitive firms. The ISI report that the number of firms using this structure is rising, and for example, of the top ten Initial Public Offerings (IPOs) in 2019, seven had dual-class share structures.

The performance effects of companies with dual-class shareholdings is inconclusive (Institutional Shareholders Service, 2019) but data from the ISS (2019) research shows that firms with dual-class share arrangements are more likely to lack independent board leadership, with roughly a half of such firms lacking an independent lead director or an independent chair on the board. In contrast, among firms without dual-class share structures only 12% lacked the same. Further, dual class firms appear to be more susceptible to experience ESG-related problems (ISS, 2019).

Dual class shares 'violate the principles of corporate democracy and the precept of "one share one vote' (Govindarajan, Rajgopal, Srivastava, and Enache, 2018: 1) but may nevertheless serve as a useful defence against short-termism. A suggestion for a middle-way is the introduction of sunset clauses, which would convert a more powerful voting stock into ordinary stock after a set period (usually between three and seven years). This is the preferred method of the Council of Institutional Investors and may indeed be the most functional way to balance the need to protect young fast-growing companies with the concern for shareholder rights.

Proposals for greater linkages between directors and shareholders have been joined by recommendations for greater connection between the board and its stakeholders, to which I turn next.

5.3 Rethinking the Board's Relationship with Stakeholders: Employee Representation

We touched on the issue of employee representation in section 2, and return to it now since here the case for reform of boards is as its strongest. Employee representation on the board is of course hardly a new or untried concept. A recent study by Lawrence (2017) showed that in 13 European countries there are significant employee representation rights in the private sector. Research on firms in Europe, both with unitary and two-tier boards, suggests that employee representation increases employee engagement (Gold, Kluge, and Conchon, 2010; Vitols, 2010). A further argument for employee representation is that it would reflect a fairer representation of the relative risks among stakeholders. Giving employees a say at board level on decisions within the company upon which they are largely dependent would strike a much better balance regarding the board's accountability to its stakeholders, and would contribute to the longer-term perspective now being so widely advocated (Lawrence, 2017; Rees, 2019; Sikka et al., 2018).

These ideas have gained recent momentum in both the USA and the UK. Senator Elizabeth Warren's proposed 2018 Accountable Capitalism Act followed the proposal of the Reward Work Act earlier in 2018, with Warren also one of the sponsors, that would allow one third of the board members in listed firms to be elected by employees.

As recently as June 2016, the then UK Prime Minister Theresa May put forward plans to have employee representatives (and consumer representatives) on company boards. The central idea was for at least two elected employees to be on the main board and the remuneration committee of firms of 250 employees or more. However, this proposal was dropped, due to considerations of practicability and the extent to which it could be carried out in a wide range of companies. Further consultation has since been sought in conjunction with the FCA (BEIS, 2017) and in January 2019 new requirements came into effect. These establish three new mechanisms for embracing employee voice within the Combined Code: a director appointed from the workforce; the creation of an employee advisory forum; or identifying a particular non-executive director who would have as part of their responsibility that employee and stakeholder views would be raised within the boardroom.

The response to this new provision from firms appears to be heavily weighted in favour of the non-executive designation option. A survey in May 2019 by LAPFF showed 73% of companies said they would choose to designate a NED, while only 5% were looking to appoint a director from the company workforce. The workforce advisory council option was the preferred route for 27% of companies surveyed (LAPFF, 2019). The primary reason for not appointing an employee director was the difficulty, for large firms, in choosing an employee who could be the representative for a wide and diverse group of employees. The non-executive option has been challenged by the trade unions in the UK, who want worker directors elected by the workforce. (TUC, 2016).

For some opponents of employee representation on the board, this is a bridge too far, and undermines the right of managers to manage. Another argument is that companies are certainly free to appoint employee representatives, and some have, such as First Direct, and John Lewis, and Capita, but the fact they don't suggests they believe it would be inefficient to do so.

These views reflect more the institutionalism inherent in both the USA and UK for the shareholder primacy perspective and the concern that if organisations depart from this, they will lose focus and become uncompetitive. But the contradictions inherent in the shareholder primacy model, and the manifest problems with the pervasive short-term approach it generates suggests change is overdue. Many people, including the UK government, have argued for customer and environmental representatives on boards. At the very least, the employees should have a place in the boardroom.

5.4 Rethinking the Board's Relationship with Stakeholders – Directors' Duties

In section 4 I mentioned the continuing debate concerning the duties of directors towards the company. The formulation of the UK Companies Act 2006 section 172 articulates the primacy of shareholders' interests with directors only required to 'have regard to' the interests of relevant stakeholders. This enlightened shareholder approach formally requires directors to consider the interests of stakeholders when making decisions but clearly does not indicate that a separate duty is to be enacted for stakeholders. There is not really a sense of balance here between shareholders and stakeholders. This is seen by the fact that it is only shareholders who can pursue legal action against a perceived breach of section 172, and not stakeholders (Keay and Loughery, 2015). Elevating stakeholders' interests to the same level as those of shareholders would ensure greater accountability and a more inclusive longer-term view of the purpose of the firm. The view has been powerfully made in recent years (e.g.

Lawrence, 2017, Sikka et al., 2018). Granting stakeholders rights under company law would be a major step forward for corporate governance.

5.5 Rethinking Board Culture

The UK corporate code has put renewed focus on the board's role in promoting a healthy culture within the organisation. It states that the board 'should establish the company's purpose, values and strategy, and satisfy itself that these and its culture are aligned. Directors must act with integrity, lead by example and promote the desired culture' (FRC, 2018: Principle B).

I mentioned 'tone from the top' in section 4, and I return to it here in the light of recent scandals which have put integrity firmly in the spotlight. A major response to such scandals by some organisations has been the introduction of an ethics committee of the board, and also, for some, the appointment of a chief ethics and compliance officer directly on the board. For example, Salesforce hired a chief ethics officer in 2018 to 'implement a strategic framework for the ethical and humane use of technology' and build 'an understanding of Salesforce's broader responsibility to their customers and society' (Salesforce, 2018).

Structural solutions such as these are fine, but my theme throughout this Element has been the emphasis on relationships. How do boards deal with executives who are dominant, and have a leadership style that is harmful to the firm? For example, in March 2019, the Hertz Corporation pursued an action against its former CEO Mark Frissora, together with a number of other directors to reclaim $70 million in bonuses and $200 million in consequential damages following the decisions by the company to restate its financial statements (Lopez, Kohn, and Mooney, 2019). The allegation against the former CEO was that his leadership style 'created a pressurised operating environment at the company,' 'demand[ed] mandatory team-wide calls and continuous weekend meetings' when told Hertz might miss a financial target and 'berate[d] subordinates' who did not come up with enough 'paradigm-busting' accounting strategies to fill the gaps,' and 'took direct and intimidating and/or demeaning steps to instil an aggressively pro-growth culture within Hertz' (Lopez, Kohn, and Mooney, 2019: para. 8).

The expected standard of conduct and style of executives is difficult territory, since the threshold between focused and aggressive commercial behaviour and insensitive, hectoring and exploitative behaviour can be open to interpretation.

Initiatives such as the Senior Managers Regime in the UK, which was intended to strengthen probity in the financial services industry after the 2008 financial crash, has sought to increase the accountability and responsiveness of the most senior staff within firms. Senior Managers must have FCA or PRA approval before starting their roles, which is recertified annually, and includes a 'statement of responsibilities' listing where their accountability lies. This statement feeds into an overall 'responsibilities map' of the organisation.

Where wrongdoing is obvious, then the board can act, but what about 'improper tone'? The lack of precise legal definition affords a large grey area here, but the board itself needs to exercise its judgement and to be able to raise any issues that appear to be troubling.

The failure to do this is highlighted clearly in recent #me-too cases. A number of examples (Steve Wynn at Wynn Casinos; Ray Kelvin at Ted Baker) showed boards tolerating patterns of behaviour of powerful leaders that were clearly unacceptable. Boards must be prepared to have bold conversations and elevated expectations for executive behaviour.

The board's behaviour should be a reflection of the values the organisation puts forward. In addition, the board should have a clear view on whether employees within the firm understand and embrace the values and the cultural norms of the organisation, and that, through the goal-setting and performance evaluation systems, managers and employees know what is expected of them, both in terms of outputs and also behaviours. In 2018, Gartner found that 87% of directors report having a good understanding of their organisation's 'tone at the top', but only 35% have a good understanding of what the culture looks like at the mid-level, and just 18% at the lower levels of the organisation (Shattuck and Carter, 2018). This is clearly not defensible.

Culture is closely linked to risk and risk appetite. The UK FRC (2018: provisions 28 and 29) states that:

> *The board should carry out a robust assessment of the company's emerging and principal risks. The board should confirm in the annual report that it has completed this assessment, including a description of its principal risks, what procedures are in place to identify emerging risks, and an explanation of how these are being managed or mitigated.*
>
> *The board should monitor the company's risk management and internal control systems and, at least annually, carry out a review of their effectiveness and report on that review in the annual report. The monitoring and review should cover all material controls, including financial, operational and compliance controls.*

The oversight of risk and promoting a strong risk culture are critical issues for the board. The requirements listed by the FRC show the extent to which boards have to be involved in culture and risk matters.

5.6 Rethinking Disruption

Many organisations are having to face the impact and implications of a range of disruptive technologies. Technology can bring widespread disruption of business models and enable a high degree of innovation. It can help organisations reach their customers in faster and better ways and it can bring greater efficiencies in markets and operations. There are dangers in being a first mover or early adopter, and there are dangers in being left behind too. Boards have to work within these parameters. The benefits of new technology are often hard to quantify and their consequences are also unclear. The board has to weigh the opportunities and risks related to disruptive technology, but in an uncertain and unpredictable environment, this is problematic. Plenty of firms have struggled to adapt to rapidly changing environments, such as Nokia, Blackberry, Kodak and Yahoo. In a recent survey (Peterson, 2020) of 826 chairs and non-executives, 41% believe their organisations were already being disrupted, compared to 31% of respondents in 2016. Boards are urged to enhance their digital competency through developing director recruitment processes or through training for directors and the board as a whole. Having digital expertise on the board is now seen as essential. For example, according to a recent MIT study (Weill, Apel, Woerner, and Banner, 2019: 41):

> *Doing business in the digital era entails risks ranging from cybersecurity breaches and privacy issues to business model disruptions and missed competitive opportunities. When a board lacks digital savvy, it can't get a handle on important elements of strategy and oversight and thus can't play its critical role of helping guide the company to a successful future.*

This means directors getting up to speed on the technology environment and how it impacts the firm, and to be able to discuss meaningfully the digital issues with management. Having expert directors on the board of course will help, particularly if there is a critical mass of them. Being 'digitally savvy' is now seen for many firms as an imperative for the board. The 'critical mass' tends to imply at least three directors who have a background either in 'a high-clock-speed industry where business models change quickly, such as software or telecom, or having an executive role with a strong technology component, such as CIO, CTO, COO, chief data officer, or, more recently, chief marketing officer' (Weill et al., 2019: 43).

In addition to skills development and continual learning for directors, there is also the issue of how much attention is given to technology in the boardroom. A recent survey of 365 public company directors highlighted concerns that not enough time was given to the emerging technology in board meetings. Only 29% of responding directors say their board discusses emerging technologies regularly. The remaining 71% say they either discuss it annually (23%) or on an ad-hoc basis (48%). Making time to discuss issues related to disruptive technologies is essential (Klemash, Lee, and Pederson, 2019).

As with digital, so too with AI. Boards are also faced with developing a coherent and effective approach to artificial intelligence (AI). For example:

> *While technology is growing exponentially, leaders and boards are only changing incrementally, leaving many legacy organisations further and further behind. It's time for leaders to courageously admit that, despite all their years of experience. AI belongs in the boardroom.* (Libert, Beck, and Bonchek, 2017: para. 16)

Boards have to decide whether and how AI can improve the functioning of the organisation and also whether and how AI can support the board in their own practices and decision-making. Because of the speed of change in technology and of course the emerging nature of the industry, board members who are knowledgeable about AI and machine learning and the Internet of Things will be hard to find. Having a Chief Technology Officer on the board, or having a Technology committee set up and report directly to the main board offers ways to increase the knowledge quotient. However, as a key subset of risks facing the business, emerging and disruptive technology requires the board as a whole to understand the strategic and operational opportunities afforded by digital, and AI, and also the risks involved. According to PWC (2018) there are some questions boards can ask management specifically about how AI will fit into the company's strategy, including:

- Have we considered how AI can transform our products or services and which aspects of our business could benefit from increased automation or machine learning?
- Have we thought about how we will use data collected by AI? Have we considered cyber risks and data privacy issues?

In addition to considering the opportunities and risks of emerging and disruptive technology for the organisation, boards should also look at the possibilities of using new approaches within the boardroom to augment strategic decision-making and to supporting the monitoring role of directors.

Where decisions need to be taken using human judgement, such as regarding strategy and vision, AI can develop possibilities that feed into the human decision-making process from which directors can choose, resulting in a better-informed process. For example, collecting data about a rapidly changing business environment, and assessing where the firm is on its trajectory, can be handled extremely well by AI, allowing directors to have better information as a basis for their decision-making. The speed at which this can be done also provides a great benefit to firms seeking to respond quickly to changes in the business landscape (Dhanrajan, 2019).

One radical thought is that AI can also improve board process regarding voice in the boardroom. I noted in section 3 that some directors are reluctant to speak up in board meetings, usually because the CEO holds too much influence. A conversation with a friend at a major technology company suggests that an AI devil's advocate may be in development, which can ask all the awkward questions in the boardroom and experience none of the potential repercussions for doing so. This could certainly help improve decision-making and may overcome of the pervasive psychological barriers to speaking up that we explored in section 3.

5.7 Conclusions: Back to Purpose

These thoughts on the board and the future suggest that current approaches to how boards are run need rethinking. I began this Element by stating two big themes.

The first is the need for boards to ensure the organisation has a clear purpose that emphasises long-term value creation and articulates the societal benefits this purpose will bring. The reports I cited in the opening section, from the Business Roundtable Statement of Purpose in the US to the 'Future of the Organisation' work sponsored by the British Academy, show a movement towards the widespread acceptance of the need for organisations to embrace corporate purpose and social impact, and with it the adoption of the stakeholder model and the prioritisation of a long-term perspective.

The reforms highlighted in this section, with the exception of the move towards a private equity model of governance, would all increase the possibility of organisations bringing greater long-term purpose and social benefits.

Of course, board reform is only one part of the answer to the question of how to get better governance. Other areas in the corporate governance landscape also have to be reviewed and changed, for example, auditor independence and the dominance of the big auditing firms, the role of financial intermediaries, tax law, insolvency law, giving priority to long-term shareholders over short-term investors, addressing the weakness of US and UK labour market regulations, dealing with the perennial embarrassment that is executive pay – these issues among many more need attention also.

The second theme is that only by balancing the structural and the relational elements of boards of directors can we truly develop ideas about improving effectiveness of the board. As Boivie and colleagues argue: 'the focus on structural characteristics of the board has caused us to overlook the need for boards to function as groups.' (Boivie et al., 2016: 347). Looking at the board as a social group focuses attention on improving the way directors are chosen, the contexts in which they interact and make decisions and how they hold each other accountable. Selecting directors from wider pools, enhancing cognitive diversity, increasing the psychological safety within boards, using technology to better communicate information within and outside the board, being more responsive to stakeholders, and giving adequate time and attention to board issues, are all ways in which the dynamics of the board would be made more effective. All these aspects may improve functioning and reduce some of the pessimism that unitary boards are inherently set up to fail. Improving the training of directors to embrace more complexity in their decision-making process, and to understand the cognitive and emotional aspects of being in such a demanding and unusual environment would undoubtedly help.

In this Element, I have focused on unitary boards of directors in corporations in the UK and the US. This is because, as we stated earlier, this form has been a test bed for theoretical and practical ideas about how organisations should be led. But there is a wide variety of other forms of governance and organisations beyond this. For example, regarding forms of governance, a good deal is known about governance systems in developed economies but there is a burgeoning literature on governance in developing economies that may have intriguing implications for how boards are run (Fainshmidt et al., 2018). With regard to different types of organisation, work on boards of entrepreneurial firms (Garg and Eisenhardt, 2017), not-for-profits (Aggarwal, Evans, and Nanda, 2012), professional service firms (Empson and Chapman 2006) and family firms (Cloyd, 2014) among others, point to the several contingencies that affect how boards operate.

The need to change boards and organisations generally has become ever more in evidence since the financial crash of 2008 and reinforced by the coronavirus outbreak in 2020. After the 2008 implosion, which provoked an economic crisis, the way companies were organised – paying large dividends to shareholders while loading up debt on their balance sheets – meant there had to be huge bailouts by the state to keep organisations running. Since 2020, in the midst of a health and economic crisis prompted by the coronavirus pandemic, the same scenario is being repeated. The speed at which companies have discovered they need help is hugely concerning. During the 2008 crash, there was a strong feeling that capitalism and in particular the shareholder primacy model needed to be reformed, or maybe even overhauled. The coronavirus pandemic has prompted similar thoughts. Leaders of businesses have long been urged to adopt greater long-term perspectives and to develop greater resilience in their firms by having higher levels of reserves in the organisation to offset risk and to increase focus on all stakeholders, not least their employees. The aftermath of the coronavirus suggests that these changes in perspective are no longer optional.

References

Acharya, A., Kehoe, C., & Reyner, M. 2008. Private equity vs PLC boards in the UK: A comparison of practices and effectiveness. *European Corporate Governance Institute*, Finance Working Paper No. 233/2009.

Aggarwal R.K., Evans, M.L., & Nanda, D. 2012. Non-profit boards: Size, performance and managerial incentives. *Journal of Accounting and Economics*, 53: 466–487.

Almandoz, J., & Tilcsik, A. 2016. When experts become liabilities: Domain experts on boards and organizational failure. *Academy of Management Journal*, 59: 1124–1149.

Barker, R. 2013. Well-trained directors are key to keeping stakeholders happy. *The Guardian*, May 30th. www.theguardian.com/sustainable-business/blog/well-trained-directors-stakeholders-happy

Baysinger, B. D., Kosnik, R. D., & Turk, T. A. 1991. Effects of board and ownership structure on corporate R&D strategy. *Academy of Management Journal*, 34: 205–214.

BBC. 2019. Barclays sees off Edward Bramson as rebel investor concedes defeat. May 2nd. www.bbc.co.uk/news/business-48133531

Bebchuk, L. A., & Fried, J. M. 2010. Tackling the managerial power problem. *Pathways*, Stanford University Press: 9–13.

Bebchuk, L. A., & Fried, J. 2004. *Pay without performance: the unfulfilled promise of executive compensation.* Cambridge: Harvard University Press.

Becker, G. 1975. *Human capital.* Columbia University Press: New York.

BEIS. 2017. *Corporate governance reform: The Government response to the Green Paper consultation*, London: Department for Business, Energy and Industrial Strategy.

Berle, A., & Means, G. 1932. *The modern corporation and private property.* Commerce Clearing House, New York.

Bertrand, M., Black, S.E., Jensen, S., & Lleras-Muney, A. 2019. Breaking the glass ceiling? The effect of board quotas on female labour market outcomes in Norway. *Review of Economic Studies*, 86: 191–239.

Bhagat, S., & Black, B. 2002. The non-correlation between board independence and long-term firm performance. *The Journal of Corporation Law*, 27: 231–274.

Bhagata, S., & Bolton, B. 2008. Corporate governance and firm performance. *Journal of Corporate Finance*, 14: 257–273.

Bjornberg, O., & Feser, C. 2015. CEO succession starts with developing your leaders. *McKinsey Quarterly*, May. www.mckinsey.com/featured-insights /leadership/ceo-succession-starts-with-developing-your-leaders

Blair. M. M., 1995. *Ownership and control: Rethinking corporate governance in the 21st century*. New York: Brookings Institution.

Blair, M. M., & Stout, L.A. 1999. A team production theory of corporate law. *Virginia Law Review*, 85: 247–328.

Blair, M. M. & Stout, L.A. 2001. Trust, trustworthiness, and the behavioural foundations of corporate law. *University of Pennsylvania Law Review*, 149: 1736–1810.

Block, D., & Gerstner, A. M. 2016. One-tier vs two-tier board structure: A comparison between the United States and Germany. Comparative corporate governance and financial regulation. Paper 1. http://scholarship .law.upenn.edu/fisch_2016/1

Boivie, S., Bednar, M. K., Aguilera, R. V., & Andrus, J. L. 2016. Are boards designed to fail? The implausibility of effective board monitoring. *Academy of Management Annals*, 10: 319–407.

Bøhren, Ø. & Staubo, S. 2016. Mandatory gender balance and board independence. *European Financial Management*, 22: 3–30.

British Academy. 2018. *The future of the corporation: Reforming business for the 21st century: A framework for the future of the corporation*. www .thebritishacademy.ac.uk/sites/default/files/Reforming-Business-for-21st-Century-British-Academy.pdf

British Private Equity and Venture Capital Association (BVCA). 2018. *Industry Activity*. www.bvca.co.uk/Research/Industry-Activity

Brown, P., & Levinson, S. C. 1987. *Politeness: some universals in language usage*. New York: Cambridge University Press.

Bullock, A. 1977. *Report of the committee of inquiry on industrial democracy* ('the Bullock Report'). Cmnd 6076, London, HMSO.

Burt, R. S. 1992. *Structural holes*. Harvard University Press: Cambridge, MA.

Business Roundtable. 2019. *Statement on the purpose of a corporation*. August 19th. https://opportunity.businessroundtable.org/wp-content/ uploads/2020/06/BRT-Statement-on-the-Purpose-of-a-Corporation-with-Signatures.pdf

Cai, J., Nguyen, T., & Walkling, R. 2020. Director Appointments – It is Who You Know. 28th Annual Conference on Financial Economics and Accounting.

Cannella, A. A., Jr., & Lubatkin, M. 1993. Succession as a socio-political process: Internal impediments to outsider selection. *Academy of Management Journal*, 36: 763–93.

Carpenter, M. A., & Westphal J. 2001. The strategic context of external network ties: examining the impact of director appointments on board involvement in strategic decision-making. *Academy of Management Journal*, 44: 639–660.

Carter, D. A., Simkins, B. J., & Simpson, G.W. 2003. Corporate governance, board diversity, and firm value. *Financial Review*, 38: 33–53.

Carter, D. A., D'Souza, F., Simkins, B. J., & Simpson, G.W. 2010. The gender and ethnic diversity of US boards and board committees and firm financial performance. *Corporate Governance: An International Review*, 18: 396–414.

Catalyst, 2020. *Women CEOs of the S&P 500*. Catalyst Research www.catalyst.org/research/women-ceos-of-the-sp-500/

Chatterjee, S., & Harrison, J. S. 2001. Corporate governance. In M. Hitt, R. E. Freeman, & J. Harrison (Eds.), *Blackwell handbook of strategic management*, 543–563. Oxford, UK: Blackwell.

Clarke, T. 2010. Recurring crises in Anglo-American corporate governance. *Contributions to Political Economy*, 29: 9–32.

Clarke, T., O'Brien, J., & O'Kelley, C. (Eds.). 2019 *The Oxford handbook of the corporation*. Oxford: Oxford University Press.

Cloyd, A. 2014. What is a board's role in a family business? *Harvard Law School Corporate Governance Forum*. July 30th. https://corpgov.law.harvard.edu/2014/07/30/what-is-a-boards-role-in-a-family-business/

Cohen, L., Frazzini, A., & Malloy, C.J. 2012. Hiring cheerleaders: board appointments of 'independent' directors. *Management Science*, 58: 1039–1058.

Coles, J. L., Daniel, N., & Naveen, L. 2014. Co-opted boards. *The Review of Financial Studies*, 27: 1751–1796.

Commonsense Principles of Corporate Governance 2.0. 2016. Millstein Centre, Columbia Law School, www.governanceprinciples.org/

Conference Board, 2019. *CEO succession practices*. Conference Board USA. www.conference-board.org/topics/ceo-succession-practices

Craig-Smith. N., & Soonieus, R. 2018. How board members really feel about ESG, from deniers to true believers. *Harvard Business Review Digital Article*. April 19th. https://hbr.org/2019/04/how-board-members-really-feel-about-esg-from-deniers-to-true-believers

Daily, C. M., Dalton, D. R., & Cannella, A.A. Jr. 2003. Corporate governance: Decades of dialogue and data. *Academy of Management Review*, 28: 371–382.

Dalton, D. R., Daily, C. M., Certo, S. T., & Roengpitya, R. 2003. Meta-analyses of financial performance and equity: Fusion or confusion? *Academy of Management Journal*, 46: 13–26.

Dalton, D. R., Daily, C. M., Ellstrand, A. E., & Johnson, J. L. 1998. Meta-analytic reviews of board composition, leadership structure, and financial performance. *Strategic Management Journal*, 19: 269–290.

Dalton. D. R., & Dalton, C. M. 2011. Integration of micro and macro studies in governance research: CEO duality, board composition, and financial performance. *Journal of Management*, 37: 404–411.

Davidson, R., Goodwin-Stewart, J., & Kent, P. 2005. Internal governance structures and earnings management. *Accounting & Finance*, 45: 241–267.

Davis, J. H., Schoorman, F. D., & Donaldson, L. 1997. Toward a stewardship theory of management. *Academy of Management Review*, 22: 20–47.

Demb, A., & Neubauer, E. F. 1992. *The corporate board: Confronting the paradoxes*. Oxford: Oxford University Press.

Deschamps, J. P. 2010. Innovation governance: How proactive is your board? *IMD Global Board Centre*. www.imd.org/contentassets/885dd6fb1a99422 bad3fd15567d41ce9/innovation-governance–how-proactive-is-your-board .pdf

Desender, K. A., Aguilera, R. V., Crespi, R., & García-Cestona, M. 2013. When does ownership matter? Board characteristics and behaviour. *Strategic Management Journal*, 34: 823–842.

Dhanrajani, S. 2019. Boardroom strategies redefined by algorithms: AI for CXO decision making. *Forbes*, March 31st.

Donaldson, L. 1990. The ethereal hand: Organisational economics and management theory. *Academy of Management Review*, 15: 369–381.

Economist, 2018. Ten years on from Norway's quota for women on corporate boards. February 17th. https://www.economist.com/business/2018/02/17/ ten-years-on-from-norways-quota-for-women-on-corporate-boards

Edmondson, A. 1999. Psychological safety and learning behaviour in work teams. *Administrative Science Quarterly*, 44: 350–383.

Ellstand, A. E., Tihanyi, L., & Johnson, J. L. 2002. Board structure and international political risk. *Academy of Management Journal*, 45: 769–777.

Eminet, A., & Guedri, Z. 2010. The role of nominating committees and director reputation in shaping the labour market for directors: An empirical assessment. *Corporate Governance: An International Review*, 18: 557–574.

Empson, L., & Chapman, C. 2006. Partnership versus corporation: Implications of alternative forms of governance in professional service firms. *Research in the Sociology of Organizations*, 24: 145–176.

Erel, I., Stern, L .H., Tan, C., & Weisbach, M. 2018. Selecting directors using machine learning. *European Corporate Governance Institute* (ECGI) – Finance Working Paper No. 605/2019.

European Trade Union Institute (ETUI). 2017. *Benchmarking working Europe*. www.etui.org/Publications2/Books/Benchmarking-Working-Europe-2017

Ezzamel, M., & Watson, R. 1997. Wearing two hats: The conflicting control and management roles of non-executive directors. In K. Keasey, S. Thompson and M. Wright (Eds.) *Corporate governance: Economic, management and financial issues*. Oxford: Oxford University Press. 54–74.

Fainshmidt, S., Judge, W.Q., Aguilera, R.V., & Smith, A. 2018, Varieties of institutional systems: A contextual taxonomy of understudied countries. *Journal of World Business*, 53: 307–322.

Fama, E. F., & Jensen, M. C. 1983. Separation of ownership and control. *Journal of Law and Economics*, 26: 301–325.

Ferrari, G., Ferraro, V., Profeta, P., & Pronzato, C. 2018. Do board gender quotas matter? Selection, performance and stock market effects. IZA Discussion Paper No. 11462.

Fich, E. M., 2005, Are some outside directors better than others? Evidence from director appointments by fortune 1000 firms. *The Journal of Business*, 78: 1943–1972.

Financial Reporting Council (FRC), 2018. *The UK corporate governance code*. London, HMSO.

Financial Reporting Council (FRC), 2018a. *Guidance on board effectiveness*. London, HMSO.

Fink, L. 2018. Letter to CEOs: A sense of purpose. *Harvard Law School Corporate Governance Forum*. January 18th. https://corpgov.law.harvard.edu /2018/01/17/a-sense-of-purpose/

Finkelstein, S., & D'Aveni, R. A. 1994. CEO duality as a double-edged sword: How boards of directors' balance entrenchment avoidance and unity of command. *Academy of Management Journal*, 37: 1079–1108.

Fogel, E. M., & Geier, A. M. 2007. Strangers in the house: Rethinking Sarbanes-Oxley and the independent board of directors. *Delaware Journal of Corporate Law*, 32: 33–72.

Forbes, D. P., & Milliken, F. J. 1999. Cognition and corporate governance: Understanding boards of directors as strategic decision-making groups. *Academy of Management Review*, 24: 489–505.

Fragale, A. R., Sumanth, J. J., Tiedens, L. Z., & Northcraft, G. B. 2012. Appeasing equals: Lateral deference in organizational communication. *Administrative Science Quarterly*, 57: 373–406.

Gardner, H. K., & Peterson, R. S. 2019. Back channels in the boardroom. *Harvard Business Review*, September-October, 106-113.

Garg, S., & Eisenhardt, K. M. 2017. Unpacking the CEO-Board relationship: How strategy-making happens in entrepreneurial firms. *Academy of Management Journal*, 60: 1828–1858.

Gill, M., Flynn, R. J. & Reissing, E. 2005. The governance self-assessment checklist: An instrument for assessing board effectiveness. *Non-profit Management and Leadership*, 15: 271–294.

Gilson, R. J., & Gordon, J. N. 2019. Board 3.0: An introduction. *The Business Lawyer*, 74: 351–366.

Gold, M., Kluge, N., & Conchon, A. 2010. *In the Union and on the board: experiences on board-level employee representatives across Europe*, Brussels: ETUI.

Govindarajan, V., Rajgopal, S., Srivastava, A., & Enache, L. 2018. Should dual-class shares be banned? *Harvard Business Review Digital Article*. March 12th: 1–6.

Guarino, A. 2017. Activist investors: More harm than good. *Global Risk Insights*, August 8th. https://globalriskinsights.com/2017/08/activist-investors-harm-good/

Guest, P. 2019. Does board ethnic diversity impact board monitoring outcomes? *British Journal of Management*, 30: 53–74.

Gupta, P. P., & Leech, T. J. 2017. *Risk oversight: Evolving expectations for boards*. Conference Board Group Governance Centre. www.fsb.org/wp-content/uploads/c_140206w.pdf

Hackman, J. R. 1987. The design of work teams. In J. Lorsch (Ed.), *Handbook of organizational behaviour*, 315–342. New York: Prentice Hall.

Hall, P. A., & Soskice, D. 2001. *Varieties of capitalism: The institutional foundations of comparative advantage*. Oxford: Oxford University Press.

Hambrick, D., Misangyi, V. F., & Park, C. A. 2015. The QUAD model for identifying a corporate director's potential for effective monitoring: Toward a new theory of board sufficiency. *Academy of Management Review*, 40: 323–344.

Hayes, R. M., & Schaefer, S. 1999. How much are differences in managerial ability worth? *Journal of Accounting and Economics*, 27: 125–148.

Hendry, J. 2002. The principals' other problems: Honest incompetence and management contracts. *Academy of Management Review*, 27: 98–113.

Hermalin, B. E., & Weisbach, M. S. 2003. Boards of directors as an endogenously determined institution: A survey of the economic literature. *Economic Policy Review*, 9: 7–26.

Hesketh, A., Sellwood-Taylor, J., & Mullen, S. 2020. Are you ready to serve on a board? *Harvard Business Review Digital Article*, January 31st. https://hbr.org/2020/01/are-you-ready-to-serve-on-a-board

Higgs Review. 2002. *Review of the role and effectiveness of non-executive directors*. Department for Business Enterprise and Regulatory Reform.

Hillman, A. J. 2005. Politicians on the board of directors: Do connections affect the bottom line? *Journal of Management*, 31: 464–481.

Hillman, A. J., Cannella, A. A., & Paetzold, R. L. 2000. The resource dependence role of corporate directors: Strategic adaptation of board composition in response to environmental change. *Journal of Management Studies*, 37: 235–256.

Hillman, A. J., & Dalziel, T. 2003. Boards of directors and firm performance: Integrating agency and resource dependence perspectives. *Academy of Management Review*, 28: 383–396.

Hillman, A. J., Shropshire, C., & Canella, A. A. 2007. Organizational predictors of women on corporate boards. *Academy of Management Journal*, 50: 941–952.

Hillman, A. 1., Withers, M., & Collins, B. J. 2009. Resource dependence theory: A review. *Journal of Management*, 35: 1404–1427.

Hodgson, P. 2009. A brief history of say on pay. Ivey Business Journal, *Ivey Business Journal*. Sep/Oct. 73: 1–1. https://iveybusinessjournal.com/publication/a-brief-history-of-say-on-pay/

Holland, T. 1991. Self-assessment by non-profit boards. *Non-profit Management and Leadership*, 2: 25–36.

Hoppman, J., Naegele, F., & Girod, B. 2019. Boards as a source of inertia: Examining the internal challenges and dynamics of boards of directors in times of environmental discontinuities. *Academy of Management Journal*, 62: 437–468.

Hoskisson, R. E., Castleton, M. W., & Withers, M. C. 2009. Complementarity in monitoring and bonding: More intense monitoring leads to higher executive compensation. *Academy of Management Perspectives*, 23: 57–74.

Houlder, D., & Nandkishore, N. 2016. Corporate governance should combine the best of private equity and family firms. *Harvard Business Review Digital Article*, December 22nd.

Huse, M. 2007. *Boards, governance and value creation: The human side of corporate governance*. Cambridge: Cambridge University Press.

Ilgen, D. R., Hollenbeck, J. R., Johnson, M., & Jundt, D. 2005. From input-process-output models to IMOI models. *Annual Review of Psychology*, 56: 517–543.

Ingley, C.B., & Van der Walt, N.T. 2001. The strategic board: the changing role of directors in developing and maintaining corporate capability. *Corporate Governance: An International Review*, 9, 174–185.

Institute of Directors (IOD), 2018. What is the role of the senior independent director? IOD Factsheet. November 15th.www.iod.com/news/news/articles/What-is-the-role-of-the-senior-independent-director

International Corporate Governance Network (ICGN). 2018. *Ensuring effective board succession planning.* www.icgn.org/ensuring-effective-board-succession-planning

Ittner, C., & Keutsch, T. 2015. The influence of board of directors' risk oversight on risk management maturity and firm risk-taking. *Management Accounting Section (MAS) Meeting.* https://papers.ssrn.com/sol3/papers.cfm?abstract_id=2482791

Institutional Shareholder Service (ISS). 2019. *ESG Review.* www.issgovernance.com/esg/

Jensen, M.C. 1989. The eclipse of the public corporation. *Harvard Business Review*, September-October, 61–74.

Jeong, S. H., & Harrison, D. A. 2016. Glass breaking, strategy making, and value creating: meta-analytic outcomes of women as CEOs and TMT members. *Academy of Management Journal*, 60: 1219–1252.

Johnson, R., & Greening, D. 1999. The effects of corporate governance and institutional ownership on corporate social performance. *Academy of Management Journal*, 42: 564–580.

Joshi, A., & Knight, A. 2015. Who defers to whom and why? Dual pathways linking demographic differences and dyadic deference to team effectiveness. *Academy of Management Journal*, 58: 59–84.

Judge, W. Q., & Zeithaml, C. P. 1992. Institutional and strategic choice perspectives on board involvement in the strategic decision process. *Academy of Management Journal*, 35: 766–794.

Kaczmarek, S., Kimino, S., & Pye, A. 2012. Antecedents of board composition: The role of nomination committees. *Corporate Governance: An International Review*, 20: 474–489.

Katzenbach, J. R., & Smith, D. K. 1993. *The wisdom of teams.* Cambridge, Harvard Business School Press.

Kay, J. 2012. *The Kay review of UK equity markets and long-term decision making.* Department for Business, Innovation and Skills, UK Government Publishing Service.

Keay, A. R., & Loughrey, J. 2015. The framework for board accountability in corporate governance. *Legal Studies*, 35: 252–279.

Kiel, G., Nicholson, G., Tunny, J.A., & Beck, J. 2012. *Directors at work: a practical guide for boards*, Thomson Reuters, Sydney, 2012.

Kiel, G. C., & Nicholson, G. 2005. Evaluating boards and directors. *Corporate Governance: An International Review*, 13: 613–631.

Kim, Y., & Canella, A. A. 2008. Toward a social capital theory of director selection. *Corporate Governance: An International Review*, 16: 282–293.

Klarner, P., Probst, G., & Useem, M. 2019. Opening the black box: Unpacking board involvement in innovation. *Strategic Organization*, 1–33. https://journals.sagepub.com/doi/pdf/10.1177/1476127019839321

Klein, K. 2017. Does gender diversity on boards really boost company performance? *Knowledge @ Wharton*, May 18th. https://knowledge.wharton.upenn.edu/article/will-gender-diversity-boards-really-boost-company-performance/

Klemash. S., Doyle, R., & Smith, J.C. 2018). Effective board evaluation. *Harvard Law School Corporate Governance Forum*. October 28th. file:///C:/Users/pstil/OneDrive/Documents/Acer%20Files/Docs/Book%20Board%20dynamics/Effective%20Board%20Evaluation%20HBS.html

Klemash, S., Lee, J., & Pederson, K. 2019. *How boards govern disruptive technology—key findings from a director survey*. EY Centre for Board Matters.

Kollewe, J. 2018. Hedge funds pressure Whitbread to spin off Costa Coffee. The Guardian, April 15th. www.theguardian.com/business/2018/apr/15/hedge-funds-pressure-whitbread-to-spin-off-costa-coffee

Kor, Y., & Misangyi, V. 2008. Outside directors' industry specific experience and firms' liability of newness. *Strategic Management Journal*, 29: 1345–1355.

Kor, Y., & Sundaramurthy, C. 2009. Experience-based human and social capital of outside directors. *Journal of Management*, 35: 981–1006.

Korn Ferry, 2017. *Three ways board members can think like activists*. Korn Ferry Institute. file:///C:/Users/pstil/OneDrive/Documents/Acer%20Files/Docs/Book%20Board%20dynamics/Activist%20Boards%20Fall%202017%20Korn%20Ferry%20.pdf

Kozlowski, S.W.J., & Bell, B.S. 2003. Work groups and teams in organizations. In W.C. Borman, D.R. Ilgen, & R.J. Klimoski (Eds.), *Handbook of psychology: Vol. 12. Industrial and organizational psychology*, 333–375. London: Wiley.

Krause, R., Semadeni, M., & Withers, M. C. 2016. That special someone: When the board views its chair as a resource. *Strategic Management Journal*, 37: 1990–2002.

Kroll, M., Walters, B. A., & Le, S. 2007. The impact of board composition and top management team ownership structure on post-IPO performance in young entrepreneurial firms. *Academy of Management Journal*, 50: 1198–1216.

Larcker, D., & Tayan, B. 2016. *Corporate governance matters*. Upper Saddle River, NJ: Pearson Education.

Lawrence, M. 2017. *Corporate governance reform. Turning business towards long-term success*. IPPR Commission on Economic Justice.

Libert, B., Beck, M., & Bonckek, M. 2017. AI in the boardroom: The next realm of corporate governance. *MIT Sloan Management Review* online, October 19th.

Lipton, M. 2019. It's time to adopt the new paradigm. *Harvard Law School Corporate Governance Forum*. February 11th. https://corpgov.law.harvard.edu /2019/02/11/its-time-to-adopt-the-new-paradigm/

Lipton, M. 2018. *The future of the corporation. Oxford University Business Law Blog*, www.law.ox.ac.uk/business-law-blog/blog/2018/11/future-corporation

Lipton, M. 2015. Risk management and the board of directors. *Harvard Law School Corporate Governance Forum*, July 28th. https://corpgov .law.harvard.edu/2015/07/28/risk-management-and-the-board-of-directors-3/

Lipton, M., Niles, S. V., & Miller, M.L. 2018. Risk management and the board of directors. *Harvard Law School Corporate Governance Forum*, March 20th. https://corpgov.law.harvard.edu/2018/03/20/risk-management-and-the-board-of-directors-5/

Local Authority Pension Fund Forum (LAPFF). 2019. *Employees on boards Modernising governance*. www.lapfforum.org/wp-content/uploads/2019/05/ LAPFFEOBSURVEY.pdf

Lopez, D., Kohn, A.H., & Mooney, M.G. 2019. Management duty to set the right 'tone at the top'. *Harvard Law School Corporate Governance Forum*, May 28th. https://corpgov.law.harvard.edu/2019/05/26/management-duty-to-set-the-right-tone-at-the-top/

Lorsch, J. W., & MacIver, E. 1989. *Pawns and potentates: The reality of America's corporate boards*. Boston: Harvard Business School Press.

Luoma, P., & Goodstein. J, 1999. Stakeholders and corporate boards: Institutional influences on board composition and structure. *Academy of Management Journal*. 42: 553–563.

Maak, T. 2007. Responsible leadership, stakeholder engagement, and the emergence of social capital. *Journal of Business Ethics*, 74: 329–343.

Magnuson, W.J. 2018. The public cost of private equity, *Minnesota Law Review*, 102: 1847–1910.

Marsh, P. 1993. *Short-termism on trial*. London: Institutional Fund Managers Association.

Marks, M. A., Mathieu, J. E., & Zaccaro, S. J. 2001. A temporally based framework and taxonomy of team processes. *Academy of Management Review*, 26: 356–376.

Martin. B. 2019. Activists target dozens of UK's biggest companies. *The Times*, July 23rd. www.thetimes.co.uk/article/activists-target-dozens-of-uk-s-big gest-companies-8ws66lpsn

Mayer, C. 2018. The future of the corporation: Towards humane business. *Journal of the British Academy*, 6(s1): 1–16.

Mayer, C. 2018a. *Prosperity: Better business makes the greater good*. Oxford: Oxford University Press.

McDonald, M. L., Westphal, J. D., & Graebner, M. E. 2008. What do they know? The effects of outside director acquisition experience on firm acquisition performance. *Strategic Management Journal*, 29: 1155–1177.

McKinsey. 2019. Private markets come of age. *McKinsey Global Private Markets Review*. www.mckinsey.com/~/Private-markets-come-of-age-McKinsey-Global-Private-Markets-Review-2019-vFashx.

McKinsey, 2016. The CEO guide to boards. *McKinsey Quarterly*, September. www.mckinsey.com/featured-insights/leadership/the-ceo-guide-to-boards

McKinsey. 2014. High-performing boards: What's on their agenda? *McKinsey Quarterly*, April. www.mckinsey.com/business-functions/strategy-and-cor porate-finance/our-insights/high-performing-boards-whats-on-their-agenda

Miller, D., Monin, T, M., & Prentice, D.A. 2000. Pluralistic ignorance and inconsistency between private and public behaviours. In D. J. Terry and M. A. Hogg (eds.), *Attitudes, Behaviour, and Social Context: The Role of Norms and Group Membership*, 95–113. Mahwah, NJ: Eribaum.

Miller, T., & Triana, M. D. C. 2009. Demographic diversity in the boardroom: mediators of the board diversity–firm performance relationship. *Journal of Management Studies*, 46: 755–786.

Miller, D. T., & McFarland, C. 1987. Pluralistic ignorance: When similarity is interpreted as dissimilarity. *Journal of Personality & Social Psychology*, 53: 298–305.

Monks, R. A. G., & Minow, N. 2011. *Corporate governance* (5th ed.). Chichester, UK: Wiley.

Moore, M. 2016. Shareholder primacy, labour and the historic ambivalence of UK company law. *University of Cambridge Faculty of Law Legal Studies Research Paper Series*, No. 40/2016.

Moos, K., & Vecchio, A. 2012. Have we placed too much faith in corporate governance reform? *Spencer Stuart, Point of View*. www.spencerstuart.com /-/media/pdf-files/research-and-insight-pdfs/pov12_indart_govrnreformnew .pdf

Morris, P., & Phalippou, P. 2020. Thirty years after Jensen's prediction: Is private equity a superior form of ownership? *Oxford Review of Economic Policy*, 36: 291–313.

Moss, J. 2016. Theresa May promises worker representatives on boards. *Personnel Today*, June 11th. www.personneltoday.com/hr/theresa-may-promises-worker-representatives-boards/

Munkholm, N.V. 2018. Board level employee representation in Europe: an overview. *Annual Conference of the European Centre of Expertise (ECE)*, Directorate General for Employment, Social Affairs and Inclusion.

NACD, 2018. *2017–2018 public company governance survey*. NACD. www.nacdonline.org/files/2017%E2%80%932018%20NACD%20Public%20Company%20Governance%20Survey%20Executive%20Summary.pdf

Nahapiet, J., & Ghoshal, S. 1998. Social capital, intellectual capital, and the organizational advantage. *Academy of Management Review*, 23: 242–266.

Nicholson, G., Kiel, G., & Tunny, J.A. 2012. Board evaluations: contemporary thinking and practice. In *Sage Handbook of Corporate Governance*. (Eds. T. Clarke, & Branson, D.M) London: Sage. 285–324.

Nicholson, G., & Newton, C. J. 2010. The role of the board of directors: Perceptions of managerial elites. *Journal of Management and Organization*, 16: 201–218.

O'Brien, D. 2008. *The private equity board: a good governance model?* London: Egon Zehnder.

Ocasio, W. 1999. Institutionalized action and corporate governance: The reliance on rules of CEO succession. *Administrative Science Quarterly*, 44: 384–416.

Parker, J. 2017. The Parker Review: A report into the ethnic diversity of UK boards. *Department for Business, Energy, and Industrial Policy*. www.gov.uk/government/publications/ethnic-diversity-of-uk-boards-the-parker-review

Parrino, R. 1997. CEO turnover and outside succession: a cross-sectional analysis. *Journal of Financial Economics*, 46: 165–197.

Peterson, R. 2020. *Predicting the unpredictable*. Harvey Nash/London Business School Annual Board Report. www.harveynash.com/group/mediacentre/AlumniHarveynashBoardResearch_2020.pdf

Pettigrew, A.M., & McNulty, T. 1995. Power and influence in and around the boardroom. *Human Relations*, 48: 845–873.

Pfeffer, J., & Salancik, G. R. 1978. *The external control of organizations: A resource dependence perspective*. New York: Harper & Row.

Pletzer, J .L., Nikolova, R., Kedzior, K. K., & Voelpe, S. C. 2015. Does gender matter? female representation on corporate boards and firm financial performance – a meta-analysis. *PLoS One*: 10 (6):e0130005. www.ncbi.nlm.nih.gov/pmc/articles/PMC4473005/

Posner, C. 2019. So long to shareholder primacy. Harvard Law School Corporate Governance Forum. August 22nd. https://corpgov.law.harvard.edu/2019/08/22/so-long-to-shareholder-primacy/

Post C., & Byron, K. 2014. Women on boards and firm financial performance: A meta-analysis. *Academy of Management Journal*, 58: 54–65.

Power, M. 1997. *The audit society. Rituals of verification*. Oxford: Oxford University Press.

Pratley, N. 2018. Putting workers on the board is a bitter but necessary pill. *The Guardian*, September 5th. www.theguardian.com/business/nils-pratley-on-finance/2018/sep/05/putting-workers-on-the-board-is-a-bitter-but-necessary-pill

PWC. 2018. *What should corporate boards know about artificial intelligence (AI)?* www.pwc.com/us/en/services/governance-insights-center/library/tech nology-hub-artificial-intelligence.html

Pye, A., & Pettigrew, A. 2005. Studying board context, process and dynamics: Some challenges for the future. *British Journal of Management*, 16: 27–38.

Rees, C. 2019. *Worker directors increasingly prominent in debates on corporate governance reform*. Involvement and Participation Association. June 3rd. www.ipa-involve.com/news/worker-directors-increasingly-prominent-in-debates-on-corporate-governance-reform

Rhee, J. 2017. A legal theory of shareholder primacy. *Minnesota Law Review*, 102: 1951–2017.

Rhoades, D. L., Rechner, P. L., & Sundaramurthy, C. 2000. Board composition and financial performance: A review and contingency model. *Journal of Managerial Issues*, 12: 76–91.

Rindova, V. P. 1999. What corporate boards have to do with strategy: a cognitive perspective, *Journal of Management Studies*, 36: 953–975.

Risso-Gill, J. 2018. It's hard to get talent on board when non-executive roles don't appeal. *Daily Telegraph*, August, 23rd. www.telegraph.co.uk/business/2018/08/23/hard-get-talent-board-non-executive-roles-dont-appeal/

Roberts, J. 2009. No one is perfect: The limits of transparency and an ethic for 'intelligent' accountability. *Accounting, Organisations and Society*. 34: 957–970.

Roberts, J. 2002. Building the complementary board: The work of the Plc chairman. *Long Range Planning*, 35: 493–520.

Roberts, J., McNulty, T., & Stiles, P. 2005. Beyond agency conceptions of the work of the nonexecutive director: Creating accountability in the boardroom. *British Journal of Management*, 16: S5–S26.

Roberts, J., & Stiles, P. 1999. The relationship between chairmen and chief executives: Competitive or complementary roles? *Long Range Planning*, 32: 36–48.

Romanelli, E., & Tushman, M. L. 1994. Organizational transformation as punctuated equilibrium: An empirical test. *Academy of Management Journal*, 37: 1141–1166.

Salesforce, 2018. Paula Goldman joins Salesforce as VP, Chief Ethical and Humane Use Officer. www.salesforce.com/news/stories/paula-goldman-joins-salesforce-as-vp-chief-ethical-and-humane-use-officer/

Schein, E. 2010. *Organizational culture and leadership*, 4th Edition. New York: John Wiley & Sons.

Schepker, D. J., Nyberg, A. J., Ulrich, M., & Wright, P. M. 2018. Planning for future leadership: Procedural rationality, formalized succession processes, and CEO influence in CEO succession planning. *Academy of Management Journal*, 61: 523–552.

Shattuck, M., & Carter, M. 2018. Future proofing the board: corporate culture on the agenda. *Teneo*, November 16th. www.teneo.com/future-proofing-the-board-corporate-culture-on-the-agenda/

Shekshina, S. 2018. How to be a good board chair. *Harvard Business Review*, March-April, 96–105.

Sikka, P., Hudson, P., Hadden, T., et al., 2018. *A better future for corporate governance: Democratising corporations for their long-term success.* http://visar.csustan.edu/aaba/LabourCorpGovReview2018.pdf

Silverstein, A., McCormack, D., & Lamm, B, 2018. The board's role in corporate social purpose. *Harvard Law School Corporate Governance Forum*, July 20th. https://corpgov.law.harvard.edu/2018/07/20/the-boards-role-in-corporate-social-purpose/

Spencer Stuart, 2019. *US Board Index*, www.spencerstuart.com/research-and-insight/us-board-index

Spencer Stuart, 2019. *UK Board Index*, www.spencerstuart.com/research-and-insight/uk-board-index

Smale, A. 2013. Progress, but still a long way to go for women in Norway. *New York Times*, June 4th.

Spira, L., & Bender, R. 2004. Compare and contrast: perspectives on board committees. *Corporate Governance: An International Review*, 12: 489–499.

Statista, 2020. Number of companies trading monthly on the London Stock Exchange from January 2015 to January 2020. www.statista.com/statistics/324547/uk-number-of-companies-lse/

Stevenson, W. B., & Radin, R. F. 2009. Social capital and social influence on the board of directors. *Journal of Management Studies*, 46: 16–44.

Stiles, P. 2001. The impact of the board on strategy: an empirical examination. *Journal of Management Studies*, 38: 627–650.

Stiles, P., & Taylor, B. 2001. *Boards at work*. Oxford: Oxford University Press.

Sundaramurthy, C., & Lewis, M. 2003. Control and collaboration: Paradoxes of governance. *Academy of Management Review*, 28: 397–415.

Tajfel, H. 1981. *Human groups and social categories: Studies in social psychology.* Cambridge: Cambridge University Press.

Terjesen, S., Aguilera, R. V., & Lorenz, R. 2014. Legislating a woman's seat on the board: Institutional factors driving gender quotas for boards of directors. *Journal of Business Ethics.* 128: 233–251

The Purposeful Company. 2018. *Intrinsic purpose definition.* The Purposeful Company Steering Group.www.biginnovationcentre-purposeful-company .com/wp-content/uploads/2019/10/tpc_intrinsic-purpose.pdf

Thuraisingham, M. 2019. *Identity, power and influence in the boardroom: Actionable strategies for developing high impact directors and boards.* London: Taylor & Francis.

Trainer, D. 2019. Verint: a tech laggard that is vastly overvalued. *Forbes,* July 24th. www.forbes.com/sites/greatspeculations/2019/07/24/verint-a-tech-laggard-that-is-vastly-overvalued/#4bb36dbb6e65

TUC. 2016. *All aboard: making worker representation on company boards a reality.* www.tuc.org.uk/sites/default/files/All_Aboard_2016.

TUC. 2014. *Beyond shareholder value: the reasons and choices for corporate governance reform.* www.tuc.org.uk/sites/default/files/BSV.pdf

Useem, M. 2006. How well-run boards make decisions. *Harvard Business Review.* November, 84: 130–138.

Vitols, S. 2010. *Board level employee representation, executive remuneration and firm performance in large European companies.* European Corporate Governance Institute and European Trades Union Institute.

Wagner, J. A., Steimpert, J. L., & Fubara, E. I. 1998. Board composition and organizational performance: Two studies of insider/outsider effects. *Journal of Management Studies,* 35: 655–677

Weill, P., Apel, T., Woerner, S. L., & Banner, J. S. 2019. It pays to have a digitally savvy board. *MIT Sloan Management Review,* 60: 41–45.

Westphal, J. D. 1999. Collaboration in the boardroom: behavioural and performance consequences of CEO-board social ties. *Academy of Management Journal,* 42: 7–24.

Westphal, J. D., & Bednar, M. K. 2005. Pluralistic ignorance in corporate boards and firms' strategic persistence in response to low firm performance. *Administrative Science Quarterly,* 50: 262–298.

Westphal, J. D., & Fredrickson, J. W. 2001. Who directs strategic change? Director experience, the selection of new CEOs, and change in corporate strategy. *Strategic Management Journal,* 22: 1113–1137.

Westphal, J. D., & Khanna, P. 2003. Keeping directors in line: Social distancing as a control mechanism in the corporate elite. *Administrative Science Quarterly,* 48: 361–398.

Westphal, J. D., & Stern, I. 2006. The other pathway to the boardroom: interpersonal influence behaviour as a substitute for elite credentials and majority status in obtaining board appointments. *Administrative Science Quarterly*, 51: 169–204.

Westphal, J. D., & Zajac, E. J. 2013. A behavioural theory of corporate governance: Explicating the mechanisms of socially situated and socially constituted agency. *Academy of Management Annals*, 7: 607–661.

Westphal, J. D., & Zajac, E. J. 1995. Who shall govern? CEO/board power, demographic similarity, and new director selection. *Administrative Science Quarterly*, 40: 60–84.

Whitley, R. 2007. *Business systems and organisational capabilities*. Oxford: Oxford University Press.

Wiersema, M., Nishimura, Y., & Suzuki, K. 2018. Executive succession: The importance of social capital in CEO appointments. *Strategic Management Journal*, 39: 1473–1495.

Williams, K.Y., & O'Reilly, C.A. 1998. Demography and diversity in organizations: A review of 40 years of research. In B.M. Staw and L.L. Cummings (Eds.), *Research in Organizational Behaviour*, Greenwich: JAI Press, 77–140.

World Economic Forum, 2016. *The new paradigm: a roadmap for an implicit corporate governance partnership between corporations and investors to achieve sustainable long-term investment and growth*. www.shareholderforum.com/access/Library/20160902_WLRK.pdf

Wu, H. 2008. How do board-CEO relationships influence the performance of new product introduction? Moving from single to interdependent explanations. *Corporate Governance; An International Review*, 16: 77–89.

Zajac, E. J., & Westphal, J. D. 1996. Who shall succeed? How CEO/board preferences and power affect the choice of new CEOs. *Academy of Management Journal*, 39: 64–90.

Zhang, Y., & Rajagopalan, N. 2004. When the known devil is better than an unknown god: An empirical study of the antecedents and consequences of relay CEO successions. *Academy of Management Journal*, 47: 483–500.

Cambridge Elements ≡

Corporate Governance

Thomas Clarke

UTS Business School, University of Technology Sydney

Thomas Clarke is Professor of Corporate Governance at the UTS Business School of the University of Technology Sydney. His work focuses on the institutional diversity of corporate governance and his most recent book is *International Corporate Governance* (Second Edition 2017). He is interested in questions about the purposes of the corporation, and the convergence of the concerns of corporate governance and corporate sustainability.

About the series

The series Elements in Corporate Governance focuses on the significant emerging field of corporate governance. Authoritative, lively, and compelling analyses include expert surveys of the foundations of the discipline, original insights into controversial debates, frontier developments, and masterclasses on key issues. Its areas of interest include empirical studies of corporate governance in practice, regional institutional diversity, emerging fields, key problems, and core theoretical perspectives.

Cambridge Elements $\overline{\overline{}}$

Corporate Governance

Elements in the series

Asian Corporate Governance: Trends and Challenges
Toru Yoshikawa

Value-Creating Boards: Challenges for Future Practice and Research
Morten Huse

Trust, Accountability and Purpose: The Regulation of Corporate Governance
Justin O'Brien

Corporate Governance and Leadership: The Board as the Nexus of Leadership-in-Governance
Monique Cikaliuk, Ljiljana Eraković, Brad Jackson, Chris Noonan and Susan Watson

The Evolution of Corporate Governance
Bob Tricker

Corporate Governance: A Survey
Thomas Clarke

Board Dynamics
Philip Stiles

A full series listing is available at: www.cambridge.org/ECG

Printed in the United States
by Baker & Taylor Publisher Services